THE BEST IN TENT CAMPING:

TENNESSEE & KENTUCKY

A Guide for Car Campers Who Hate RVs, Concrete Slabs, and Loud Portable Stereos

Other Books by Johnny Molloy

Trail by Trail: Backpacking in the Smoky Mountains
Day & Overnight Hikes in the Great Smoky Mountains National Park
Best in Tent Camping: Southern Appalachian & Smoky Mountains
Best in Tent Camping: Florida
Day & Overnight Hikes in Shenandoah National Park
Beach & Coastal Camping in Florida
Best in Tent Camping: Colorado
A Paddler's Guide to Everglades National Park
Day & Overnight Hikes in West Virginia's Monongahela National Forest
Best in Tent Camping: West Virginia
The Hiking Trails of Florida's National Forests, Parks, and Preserves
Mount Rogers Outdoor Recreation Handbook
Long Trails of the Southeast
From the Swamp to the Keys: A Paddle Through Florida History
60 Hikes Within 60 Miles: Nashville
Land Between The Lakes Outdoor Recreation Handbook

Visit the author's website: www.johnnymolloy.com

THE BEST IN TENT CAMPING:

TENNESSEE & KENTUCKY

A Guide for Car Campers Who Hate RVs, Concrete Slabs, and Loud Portable Stereos

1st Edition

Johnny Molloy

Menasha
Ridge
Press

This book is for my sister-in-law, Julie.

Copyright © 2002 by Johnny Molloy
All rights reserved
Printed in the United States of America
Published by Menasha Ridge Press
Distributed by the Globe Pequot Press
First edition, second printing 2004

Cataloging-in-Publication Data is available from the Library of Congress.

ISBN 0-89732-370-X

Cover design by Grant Tatum
Cover photo copyright Pat O'Hara/Corbis

Menasha Ridge Press
P.O. Box 43673
Birmingham, Alabama 35243
www.menasharidge.com

CONTENTS

TENNESSEE CAMPGROUNDS

Western Tennessee

Middle Tennessee

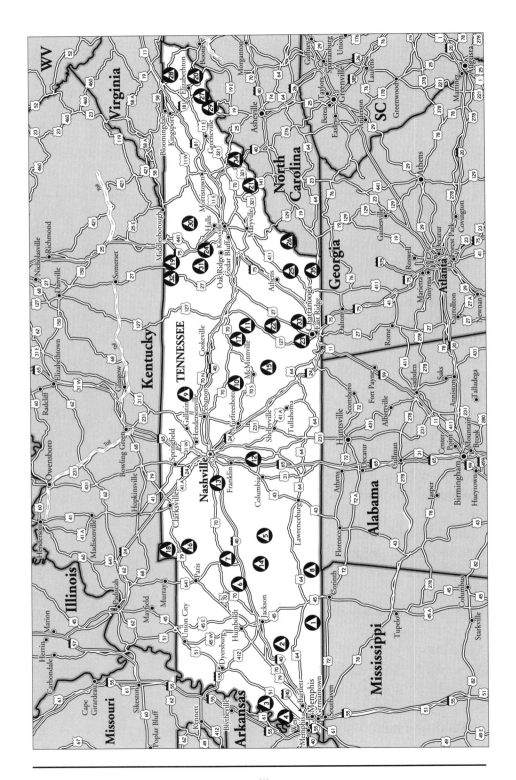

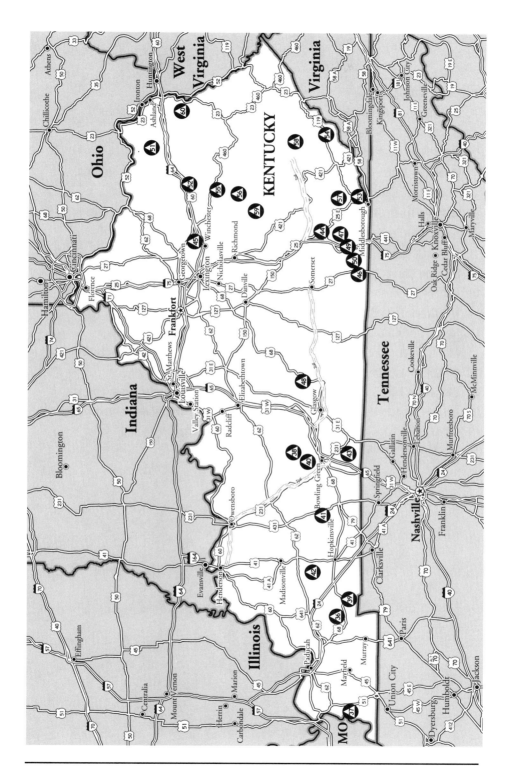

Tennessee Campgrounds
1. Big Hill Pond State Park
2. Chickasaw State Park
3. Fort Pillow State Historic Park
4. Meeman-Shelby State Park
5. Meriwether Lewis Monument
6. Natchez Trace State Park and Forest
7. Nathan Bedford Forrest State Park
8. Pickwick Landing State Park
9. Bledsoe Creek State Park
10. Cedars of Lebanon State Park
11. Fall Creek Falls State Park
12. Henry Horton State Park
13. Montgomery Bell State Park
14. Mousetail Landing State Park
15. Old Stone Fort State Archeological Park
16. Piney
17. Rock Island State Park
18. Rushing Creek
19. Bandy Creek Campground
20. Cardens Bluff
21. Cosby Campground
22. Foster Falls Recreation Area
23. Franklin State Forest
24. Frozen Head State Park
25. Gee Creek Campground
26. Holly Flats Campground
27. Limestone Cove
28. Little Oak Campground
29. Nolichucky Gorge
30. Norris Dam State Park
31. Obed Wild and Scenic River
32. Pickett State Park
33. Prentice Cooper State Forest
34. Round Mountain Campground
35. Sylco Campground

Kentucky Campgrounds

MAP LEGEND

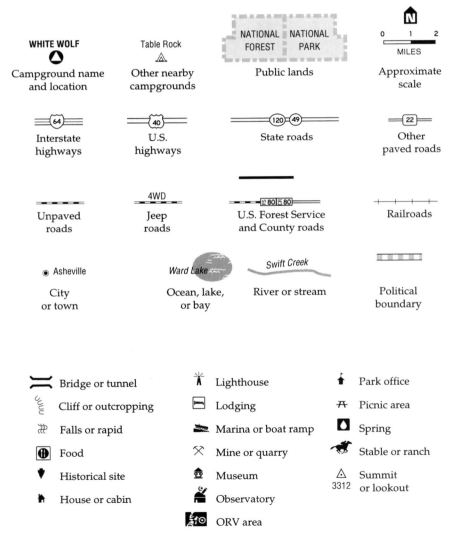

WHITE WOLF
Campground name
and location

Table Rock
Other nearby
campgrounds

NATIONAL NATIONAL
FOREST   PARK
Public lands

Approximate
scale
MILES
0   1   2

64
Interstate
highways

40
U.S.
highways

120 49
State roads

22
Other
paved roads

Unpaved
roads

4WD
Jeep
roads

80 80
U.S. Forest Service
and County roads

Railroads

Asheville
City
or town

Ward Lake
Ocean, lake,
or bay

Swift Creek
River or stream

Political
boundary

Bridge or tunnel

Cliff or outcropping

Falls or rapid

Food

Historical site

House or cabin

Lighthouse

Lodging

Marina or boat ramp

Mine or quarry

Museum

Observatory

ORV area

Park office

Picnic area

Spring

Stable or ranch

3312 Summit
or lookout

ACKNOWLEDGMENTS

I would like to thank the following people for helping me in the research and writing of this book: All the land managers of Kentucky and Tennessee's state parks, the folks at Land Between the Lakes, Cherokee and Daniel Boone National Forests, Mammoth Cave National Park, Smoky Mountains National Park, and the lakes administered by the Army Corps of Engineers.

Thanks to Lisa Daniel for camping with me and keeping me company on and off the trail, to my Mom in Memphis, and to Jason Money and Karen Stokes for exploring the Big South Fork with me. Thanks to Linda Grebe at Eureka for providing me the Mountain Pass X2, a great tent for camping; to Silva compasses; and to Camp Trails for their Wilderness pack. Thanks to Jean Cobb and Brooke Wilson at Freebairn & Co., Slumberjack for a good sleeping bag and sleeping mat to enable a good night's rest.

The biggest thanks of all goes to the people of my native Tennessee, and to my neighbors in Kentucky who love their homeland as much as I love mine.

PREFACE

Being a native Tennessean and lover of the outdoors, I thought I had a leg up on writing this book, knowing all I already knew about the Volunteer State as well as its neighbor, Kentucky. What I ended up learning is that there is a lot more out there than I thought! In early spring, I set forth in my Jeep, with a Eureka! tent and a laptop computer, exploring by day and typing up on-site reports by night. The first surprise came in West Tennessee at the Civil War site of Fort Pillow State Park. Not only did it offer a view of the Mississippi River from a steep bluff rivaling any mountain vista, but it had one of the finest campgrounds in this book! Next, I headed east to Nathan Bedford Forrest State Park, a jewel on the Tennessee River with vistas from on high and a riverside campground. As I moved on toward Middle Tennessee, water continued as a theme. I admired the waterfalls at Old Stone Fort and Rock Island State Parks. Fall Creek Falls is renown for its cascades, but new walk-in tent sites clinched it as a premier destination. More water awaited me as I continued east, as the Obed National Wild and Scenic River added a high-quality tent campground.

When summer arrived, I headed for the hills of East Tennessee, where places like Cardens Bluff and the high country campgrounds like Round Mountain kept me cool. I also learned the Civil War is a big part of Kentucky's history. I stood atop incredible river bluffs of the state's "Far West," overlooking the Mississippi River and the state of Missouri where Confederate soldiers were once stationed behind fortifications. Eventually I returned to water at the Land Between the Lakes. One of America's newest national recreation areas, administered by the U.S. Forest Service, "LBL" is simply a tent camper's paradise. Nearly encircled by lakes, laced with trails, rich with wildlife and a pioneer past, this destination, shared with Tennessee, has a number of campgrounds to enjoy. Other lakes shone in the Bluegrass State: Lake Malone, Green River Lake, and Nolin River Lake. Each offered waterfront camps that didn't fail to please. Mammoth Cave National Park is one of the places not to be missed. Farther east, the Daniel Boone National Forest offers numerous getaways in the deep forests known in Daniel Boone's time as the "Great Wilderness." Some, like Red River Gorge, are famed, others, such as Turkey Foot, are hidden gems. The Big South Fork and Cumberland Gap are destinations shared by the two states that are special enough to be administered by the National Park Service. Not to be overlooked is Yatesville Lake State Park, with its state-of-the-art campground.

The days began to shorten—fall was on its way—and with the joy of completing a book and the sadness of an adventure ended, I finished my research. However, I continued putting my lessons to work, enjoying more of these two fantastic states, fishing the Duck River, hiking at Mammoth Cave, and paddling the Obed watershed. I am very grateful and proud to call this area home, so I can enjoy the best of Kentucky and Tennessee for a lifetime of outdoor adventure.

—*Johnny Molloy*

INTRODUCTION

A Word about This Book and Tennessee & Kentucky Tent Camping

Kentucky and Tennessee are two of the oldest states west of the Appalachian Mountains. Settled by pioneers such as Daniel Boone and James Winchester, the Volunteer State and the Bluegrass State are steeped in American history, from the settler's passage at Cumberland Gap to Daniel Boone's Fort Boonesborough to the Civil War's Fort Pillow. Pioneers traveled on rough overland trails and along rivers used for passage through the vast forests that thrived in their interiors. These high, rich mountains, including the Appalachians and the Cumberland Plateau, still form a rampart to settlement and now offer preserved destinations. Farther west are "barrens," areas in the forests that Indians kept open to attract game to hunt. The Ohio and Mississippi rivers form the state's western borders and are their respective lowest elevations.

Today tent campers can enjoy these parcels, each pieces of distinct regions of Kentucky and Tennessee. In West Tennessee, you can explore the surprisingly hilly terrain of Big Hill Pond, on the Mississippi border. Middle Tennessee is the land of unique cedar glades where unusual plants and animals still thrive and where the water falls from the western Cumberland Plateau. East Tennessee has the highest of the high, including the crest of the Appalachians, where elevations in the Smoky Mountains exceed 6,000 feet. Eastern Kentucky has its high points, too, such as Kingdom Come State Park that offers far-reaching mountain views. The rugged terrain of the Daniel Boone National Forest covers both Eastern and Central Kentucky. Rock bluffs overlook gorges cut by water and time. This is also lake country, where reservoirs built to prevent disastrous flooding are now recreation destinations. Western Kentucky is pocked with caves and is home to Kentucky Lake and Lake Barkley, which together from the second largest manmade body of water in the world. This vast watershed encircles Land Between the Lakes.

All this spells paradise for the tent camper. No matter where you go, the scenery will never fail to please the eye. Before embarking on a trip, take time to prepare. Many of the best tent campgrounds are a fair distance from the civilized world, and you want to enjoy yourself rather than make supply or gear runs. Call ahead and ask for a park map, brochure, or other information to help you plan your trip. Visit websites. Make reservations wherever applicable, especially at popular state parks. Ask questions. Ask more questions. The more

questions you ask, the fewer surprises you will get. There are other times, however, when you'll grab your gear and this book, hop in the car, and just wing it.
This can be an adventure in its own right.

The rating system

Included in this book is a rating system for Kentucky and Tennessee's 50
best tent campgrounds. Certain campground attributes—beauty, site privacy,
site spaciousness, quiet, security, and cleanliness/upkeep—are ranked using
a star system. Five stars are ideal, one is acceptable. This system will help you
find the campground that has the attributes you desire.

Beauty

In the best campgrounds, the fluid shapes and elements of nature—flora,
water, land, and sky—have melded to create locales that seem to have been
made for tent camping. The best sites are so attractive you may be tempted
not to leave your outdoor home. A little site work is all right to make the
scenic area camper-friendly, while too many reminders of civilization elimi-
nated many a campground from inclusion in this book.

Site privacy

A little understory goes a long way in making you feel comfortable once
you've picked your site for the night. There is a trend in planting natural borders between campsites if the borders don't exist already. With some trees or
brush to define the sites, everyone has their personal space. Then you can go
about the pleasures of tent camping without keeping up with the Joneses at
the site next door—or they with you.

Site spaciousness

This attribute can be very important depending on how much of a gear-
head you are and the size of your group. Campers with family-style tents
need a large, flat spot on which to pitch their tent and still to get to the ice

chest to prepare foods, all the while not getting burned near the fire ring. Gearheads need adequate space to show all their stuff off to neighbors strolling by. I just want enough room to keep my bedroom, den, and kitchen separate.

Quiet

The music of the mountains, rivers, and all the land between—the singing birds, rushing streams, wind whooshing through the trees—includes the kinds of noises tent campers associate with being in Kentucky and Tennessee. In concert, they camouflage the sounds you don't want to hear—autos coming and going, loud neighbors, and so on.

Security

Campground security is relative. A remote campground with no civilization nearby is usually safe, but don't tempt potential thieves by leaving your valuables out for all to see. Use common sense and go with your instinct. Campground hosts are wonderful to have around, and state parks with locked gates are ideal for security. Get to know your neighbors and develop a buddy system to watch each other's belongings when possible.

Cleanliness/upkeep

I'm a stickler for this one. Nothing will sabotage a scenic campground like trash. Most of the campgrounds in this guidebook are clean. More rustic campgrounds—my favorites—usually receive less maintenance. Busy weekends and holidays will show their effects; however, don't let a little litter spoil your good time. Help clean up, and think of it as doing your part for Kentucky and Tennessee's natural environment.

Helpful Hints

To make the most of your tent-camping trip, call ahead whenever possible. If going to a state or national park, call for an informative brochure before setting out. This way you can familiarize yourself with the area. Once there, ask questions. Most stewards of the land are proud of their piece of terra firma and are honored you came for a visit. They're happy to help you have the best time possible.

If traveling to the Cherokee National Forest or Daniel Boone National Forest, call ahead and order a forest map. Not only will a map make it that much easier to reach your destination, but nearby hikes, scenic drives, waterfalls, and landmarks will be easier to find. There are forest visitor centers in addition to ranger stations. Call or visit and ask questions. When ordering a map, ask for any additional literature about the area in which you are interested.

In writing this book I had the pleasure of meeting many friendly, helpful people: local residents proud of the unique lands around them, state park and national forest employees who endured my endless questions. Even better were my fellow tent campers, who were eager to share their knowledge about their favorite spots. They already know what beauty lies on the horizon. As these Southern states become more populated, these lands become that much more precious. Enjoy then, protect them, and use them wisely.

WESTERN
TENNESSEE

BIG HILL POND STATE PARK

Selmer

This is the best-kept secret in Western Tennessee. On the brink of closure after budget battles in Nashville, Big Hill Pond State Park survived because of its wetlands, which lie in the flood plain of the Tuscumbia River. But this park is not all about wetlands, for Big Hill Pond mostly has steep hills broken with rock outcrops hovering over sharp wooded ravines. A walk on any of the 30 miles of trails here will testify to that. The entire trail system, with loop possibilities ideal for day hikers, is special enough to have been designated a National Recreation Trail. And when darkness comes, you will find that the campground was seemingly designed with tent campers in mind.

The 30-site campground is set on a ridge above Dismal Branch. This rolling backdrop offers vertical variation to your camping opportunities. Enter a classic campground loop shaded by tall pines, hickories, and oaks. Campsites are made level in this hilly country by landscaping timbers. The first few sites are the most open and sunny, if that is your preference. The other campsites are shaded by dense woods.

Smaller trees form a thick understory. Campsite size is ample for your average tent camper and gear. Campsite privacy, while excellent, isn't much of an issue, as this undiscovered getaway is rarely crowded. As you continue around the

CAMPGROUND RATINGS

Beauty:	★★★★★
Site privacy:	★★★★★
Site spaciousness:	★★★
Quiet:	★★★★★
Security:	★★★★★
Cleanliness/upkeep:	★★★★★

This is the most underused and under-appreciated state park in Western Tennessee.

WESTERN

loop, a small side road has a few pull-through sites.

An intermittent streambed runs alongside the second half of the loop. There are more dogwoods and pines here. Make a final climb past some sites that are a little close together, and complete the loop. A fully equipped bathhouse lies in the center of the loop, along with a couple of campsites. The campground is in the heart of the park, which gives it an honest sense of being in the real, natural Tennessee. Spring and fall are the more popular seasons, but even then Big Hill Pond very rarely fills.

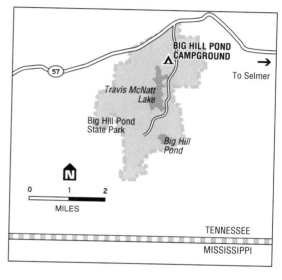

The origin of Big Hill Pond was an 1853 railroading venture. Fill dirt was used to create a levee across Tuscumbia and Cypress Creeks, and the resulting hole filled with water. A newer impoundment, Travis McNatt Lake, is a more recent recreational centerpiece. Both lakes offer fishing, but Big Hill Pond is a little harder to reach, whereas Travis McNatt Lake is just a short piece from the campground. Spring fed and 165 acres in size, Big Hill Pond is full of bass, bream, and catfish. Even if you don't catch anything, the "no gas motors" lake is a pleasure to paddle in a canoe, especially in spring, when the azaleas are blooming, or when autumn's paintbrush reflects off the water.

A 30-mile trail system explores the high and the low of Big Hill, including Pond's natural offerings as well as a little Civil War history—some earthworks built by Union soldiers for protecting the railroad. The highest of the high is an observation tower where there are 360° views of the surrounding countryside and far south into Mississippi, across the Tuscumbia River Valley. The lowest of the low is the 0.8-mile boardwalk traversing Dismal Swamp, a bottomland forest that attracts water-fowl and other wildlife. In between are wooded hills and surprisingly steep valleys. Don't be astonished if you see deer on the ridges and waterfowl in the lake or hear turkeys gobble in the unseen distance. The narrow paths meander over clear streams on small foot bridges and past old homesites where subsistence farmers once eked out a living. You will see Mother Nature thriving here in a much richer fashion.

To get there: From Selmer, head south on US 45 for 7 miles to TN 57. Turn right and head west on 57 for 10 miles to the Big Hill Pond entrance, which will be on your left.

CHICKASAW STATE PARK

Henderson

Of the 14,000-plus acres found in Chickasaw State Park and the surrounding Chickasaw State Forest, over 1,200 have been set aside for recreational use. Fortunately for us, a picturesque, hilly section alongside the park's Lake Placid has been set aside for tent campers. Lake Placid offers water activities just a walk away, while horse, hiking, and motor trails spill out from the state park into the adjacent state forest, offering plenty of avenues to roam about.

Just past the campground entrance is the camp store, open during summer. Across from the store is the Trailer Camp, located hillside in tall pine woods with occasional cedars and hardwoods. A thin understory with some grass is offset by decent spacing between campsites. Trailer Camp is divided into two loops with bathhouses in the center of each. The pull-ins at many sites are so sloped as to render them nearly unusable by an RV. Tent campers who want electricity will seek these sites. A campground host is located here for your safety and convenience.

Beyond Trailer Camp is Wrangler Camp, the only campground open year-round. It is located below the Lake Placid dam. Non-equestrians can use this area only during winter, when the other camps are closed. The sites are well spaced and open, with some shade rendered by tall pines and a few cypress trees. Grass carpets the

CAMPGROUND RATINGS

Beauty:	★★★★
Site privacy:	★★★★
Site spaciousness:	★★★
Quiet:	★★★★
Security:	★★★★★
Cleanliness/upkeep:	★★★★★

Stay at a lakeside tent camp and enjoy the varied recreation opportunities.

WESTERN

campground floor. Wrangler Camp has its own bathhouse as well.

Located on the south shore of the impoundment fed by Piney Creek, Lake Placid Tent Camp is the preferred destination for readers of this book. Pine, oak, and hickory trees cover the vertically varied woodland. Sites are widely spread along a ridge-running road leading toward the water. Shady hollows flank the ridgeline. Some sites have circular picnic tables. A fully equipped bathhouse stands

in the center of an auto turnaround. On the outside of the turnaround are several large, attractive sites that overlook the lake. Landscaping timbers have been used to level the campsites.

A side road spurs off the turnaround and leads down to the lake. Attractive, though smaller sites with lake views are spread along both sides of this road. There are a couple of sites directly on the lake just before the road dead-ends at a foot bridge spanning Lake Placid. Water spigots are spread throughout the campground.

Once camp has been set up, there is plenty to do. The Lakeshore Nature Trail runs right beside the tent camp, and if you want to take a dip in the lake, cross the footbridge over to the swim beach. The clear, cool lake is inviting during the summertime. High-dive and low-dive boards add a little zing to swimmer's water entrances. Paddle boats and rowboats are available for rent, but no private boats are allowed. Many folks choose to wet a line from the bank or a boat, vying for bass and bluegill.

If you want to stay on land, hike the Forked Pine Nature Trail, which leaves from near the picnic shelters. If horseback riding is your thing, an on-site equestrian stable leads trail rides. Beyond the park recreation area, the state forest has over 50 miles of gravel roads and trails for horse, hikers, mountain bikers, and autos. A forest map is available at the park office. All they ask is to stay on the established paths and roads.

Chickasaw also has a more developed side, with tennis, basketball, and volleyball courts, horseshoe pits, an archery range, and playgrounds. Parents will be glad to know that during summer a park recreation director keeps kids busy with arts, crafts, games, movies, and evening programs. The recreation opportunities at Chickasaw run the gamut, so you shouldn't suffer from boredom here, just remember to throw in a little relaxation while you're at it.

To get there: From Henderson, head west on TN 100 for 10 miles to the entrance of Chickasaw State Park, which will be on your left.

KEY INFORMATION

**Chickasaw State Park
20 Cabin Lane
Henderson, TN 38340**

Operated by: Tennessee State Parks

Information: (901) 989-5141, www.tnstateparks.com

Open: RV and Lake Placid Tent Camp, mid-March–November; Wrangler Camp, year-round

Individual sites: 121 sites

Each site has: Lake Placid Tent Camp has picnic table, lantern post, upright grill, fire ring; Trailer Camp and Wrangler Camp have water, electricity, picnic table, upright grills, fire ring

Site assignment: First come, first served; no reservation

Registration: Ranger will come by and register you

Facilities: Hot showers, water spigots

Parking: At campsites only

Fee: Lake Placid Tent Camp $11 per night; Trailer Camp and Wrangler Camp $17 per night

Elevation: 480 feet

Restrictions

Pets—On 6-foot leash only

Fires—In fire rings only

Alcoholic beverages—Not allowed

Vehicles—Maximum 2 vehicles per site

Other—14-day stay limit

FORT PILLOW STATE HISTORIC PARK
Covington

Simply put, I love this campground. Why, you ask? It has everything that a tent camper could desire: well-designed sites in an attractive wooded setting; above-average campsite spaciousness and privacy; lots of outdoor activities in which to indulge; and an abundant number of sites that rarely fill. After seeing this campground on an ideal Friday evening, I was shocked to see a mere one tent staked out!

Enter the campground, which is divided into three loops. The upper loop occupies the highest spot on a hill. It is heavily wooded, yet is the least wooded of the three loops. Hickory, maples, and oak trees shade the spacious and well-spaced sites. Grass covers much of the loop. The apex of the loop has sites that look out over the Mississippi River through the trees. A fully equipped bathhouse stands in the center of the loop.

The middle loop has more big trees, especially beech trees, and offers vertical variation among steep wooded ravines. The loop road winds closely among these trees. Attractive, well-separated campsites lie on the edge of these drop-offs. The hills add to already superlative campsite privacy. Water spigots are adequately spaced about here, as they are in the whole campground. The south loop shows that the situation can get even better. This loop is for tenters only. Many of these sites are walk-ins that have even more solitude. I recom-

CAMPGROUND RATINGS

Beauty:	★★★★★
Site privacy:	★★★★★
Site spaciousness:	★★★★
Quiet:	★★★★★
Security:	★★★★★
Cleanliness/upkeep:	★★★★★

Fort Pillow has one of the best campgrounds in this entire guidebook.

WESTERN

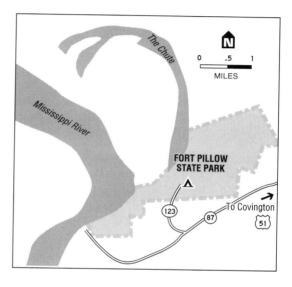

mend this loop above the others, though there is not a bad site in the campground.

Fort Pillow fills only during special events, such as Civil War reenactments. Other than that you can get a site any weekend of the year. The bugs can be troublesome at certain times. Call the park office ahead of time to address this potential concern.

As with many state parks in the South, action during the Civil War at this site has led to its preservation as both a historical and natural area. The natural is impressive—Fort Pillow is located on the Chickasaw Bluffs overlooking the Mississippi River. The Mighty Mississip' once ran to the edge of the bluffs, before the river changed course and now runs farther away. The old route of the river is now an oxbow lake and is known as The Chute. Back in 1861, the Confederate Army built extensive fortifications here to defend the river. The year 1862 saw a gun battle nearby, and later the Union bombarded Fort Pillow, which ultimately resulted in its being abandoned by the Confederates and occupied by Union forces. In 1864, Nathan Bedford Forrest himself attacked the fort. The Rebels carried the day and Forrest asked for surrender, but the Feds refused. Subsequently, the Confederates stormed Fort Pillow and overwhelmed the Union and won the battle. Afterwards, both sides abandoned the fort.

Today you can walk the half-mile trail to the fort, in addition to other major interpretive trails. For a better understanding of the battle, an interpretive center has a video, artifacts, and other memorabilia on display. There are also interpretive programs and special events at the park during summer, where visitors can learn about a soldier's life and weapons of the Civil War, go on an owl prowl, or enjoy nature walks. Spring and fall see a Civil War living history and discovery, where folks act out life back then and also participate in reenactments. Call the park office for exact dates.

Two loop trails accommodate campers who want to tour the actual grounds of the area that drew attention from both sides. The inner loop runs for 3.8 miles and the outer loop runs for 7.8 miles along earthen fortifications and through surprisingly challenging terrain. In addition, there is the five-mile, one-way Chickasaw Bluffs Trail that attracts many backpackers. Less strenuous activities include boating and fishing on 15-acre Fort Pillow Lake, where bass, bream, and crappie await your rod. Other nearby attractions include the home of Alex Haley, author of Roots, in nearby Henning, and the Lower Hatchie National Wildlife Refuge, just south of Fort Pillow. No matter what you do, save some time for the campground. It is a good one.

KEY INFORMATION

Fort Pillow State Park
3122 Park Road
Henning, TN 37841

Operated by: Tennessee State Parks

Information: (731) 738-5581, www.tnstateparks.com

Open: Year-round

Individual sites: 40

Each site has: Picnic table, fire ring, tent pad

Site assignment: First come, first served; no reservation

Registration: Ranger will come by and register you

Facilities: Hot showers, flush toilets, water spigots, laundry

Parking: At campsites only

Fee: $7 per night

Elevation: 420 feet

Restrictions:

Pets—On 6-foot leash only

Fires—In fire rings only

Alcoholic beverages—Not allowed

Vehicles—None

Other—14-day stay limit

To get there: From the junction of TN 54 and US 51 in Covington, head north on US 51 for 8.5 miles to TN 87. Turn left on TN 87 and follow it for 17 miles to TN 123, Old Fulton Road. Turn right on TN 123 and follow it for 1 mile to the state park.

MEEMAN-SHELBY STATE PARK

Millington

The Mississippi River made Memphis, so it is only fitting that a nearby getaway lies on the banks of the Father of Waters. What surprises visitors are the outdoor opportunities—hiking, biking, and paddling—in a serene park that is so close to downtown. (We're talking 15 miles as the crow flies.) Located north of the city on the Chickasaw Bluffs, this park was first developed by the National Park Service and later deeded to the state of Tennessee. It is a good 10° cooler here in the summer than it is in Memphis, mostly due to the tall trees of this 14,000-acre preserve.

Dogwood Ridge Campground, your base camp, lies beneath a tall deciduous forest of sugar maple, tulip trees, and sweetgum. It is divided into three loops. Smaller trees create adequate campsite privacy. The campsites are level, even though the terrain falls away from the campground. Come to the first loop. The first five campsites are the only ones that can be reserved. The spacious sites are well spaced apart from one another as well. The second loop spurs off the first loop. Here, younger trees grow among the shade-bearing giants overhead. Pass a fully equipped bathhouse and return to the first loop. Keep passing nice campsites and come to the third loop. This final loop is the best in this well-groomed, well-cared-for area. The many dogwood trees here may account for the campground name. Since there are water and electrical

CAMPGROUND RATINGS

Beauty:	★★★★
Site privacy:	★★★★
Site spaciousness:	★★★★
Quiet:	★★★★
Security:	★★★★
Cleanliness/upkeep:	★★★★★

This wooded getaway is a world apart from nearby Memphis.

WESTERN

hookups, there will be some big rigs here, but don't let this deter you. Remember, this place was attractive enough for the National Park Service to develop before they deeded it over to the state of Tennessee. Meeman-Shelby fills during special events in nearby Memphis and on summer holiday weekends. Other than that you should be able to get a campsite. If you have any worries, just reserve a site.

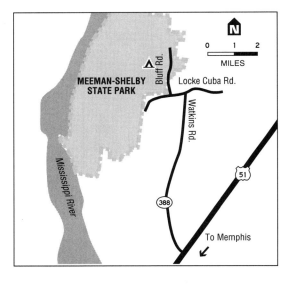

The vast forests will be the first surprise. Steep-sided ravines dissect the Chickasaw Bluffs where large beech, tulip, and sycamore trees grow. Towering oaks thrive on the higher ground. Giant cottonwoods grow near the river. There are 20 miles of trails to explore. The Chickasaw Trail runs eight miles along the western edge of Chickasaw Bluff, spanning streams flowing to the Mississippi. Keep an eye for plentiful wildlife, such as hawks, beaver, and raccoons. The Woodland Trail winds along creeks and past small oxbow lakes in a big forest. The Pioneer Springs Trail passes a historic water source used by the Chickasaw Indians and settlers alike, as it cruises along the base of the bluffs. Mountain bikers can ply the Bicycle Trail, which makes a five-mile car-free trek. Both paved and gravel roads offer other pedaling opportunities.

What has caught on lately is sea kayaking the Mississippi River. Paddlers drop their boats into the swift water and cruise the scenic shoreline. One trip requiring a shuttle heads downstream from Meeman-Shelby 18 miles to Mud Island. Along the way are sandbars in excess of 100 acres that make for riverine beachcombing.

As if the mighty Mississippi River isn't water enough for campers, there is also Poplar Tree Lake. Its 125 acres offer angling for bass, bream, and catfish. A fishing pier is available if you're without a boat, or you can rent a boat on the spot. If you own a boat, remember, only electric motors are allowed, which makes for a quieter, more pleasant fishing experience. A smaller body of water provides a good swimming pool, open during summer months. An unusual pastime here is playing Frisbee golf. Bring your disc and try your hand on the 18-hole course. Other outdoor games are possible, including badminton and volleyball. So many choices, so little time—you might have to spend an extra day or two here getting all the fun in.

KEY INFORMATION

Meeman-Shelby State Park
910 Riddick Road
Millington, TN 38053

Operated by: Tennessee State Parks

Information: (901) 876-5215, www.tnstateparks.com

Open: Year-round

Individual sites: 49

Each site has: Picnic table, fire ring, upright grills, water, electricity

Site assignment: First come, first served; some reservation

Registration: Park Visitor Center

Facilities: Hot showers, flush toilets

Parking: At campsites only

Fee: $14 per night for tent campers; $16 per night for all others

Elevation: 350 feet

Restrictions:

Pets—On 6-foot leash only

Fires—In fire rings only

Alcoholic beverages—Not allowed

Vehicles—None

Other—14-day stay limit

To get there: From I-240 on exit 2A in north Memphis, drive north a short distance to US 51. Head north on US 51 for 4 miles to Watkins Road, TN 388. Turn left on 388 and follow it 7 miles to Locke Cuba Road. Turn left on Locke Cuba Road and follow it 0.5 mile to Bluff Road. Turn right on Bluff Road to enter the park.

MERIWETHER LEWIS MONUMENT

Columbia

This is one campground you will want to take your time heading to, reaching it by way of the historic Natchez Trace Parkway. When I visited, I came from Nashville, stopping at the many roadside sights along the way. After spending time here, I was ashamed I hadn't visited before. In addition to the interesting human and natural history, as well as free camping, the nearby Buffalo River offers one of the finest canoe float trips in the state.

The campground lies on a ridgetop in young oak-hickory woods. Steep hillsides drop off from all sides of the camping area. Younger trees separate the sites, which are well maintained, well spaced, and offer decent privacy. The campground is broken into one loop and a side road. The main loop is on a wide ridgeline and offers good sites, most of which lie on the outside of the loop, offering woodland views. The side-road area lies on a narrow ridge, with sites strung along its length. Each site has a good view into the woods below. A small auto turnaround at the end of the road offers a few more sites, and they are the quietest of all.

There is a water spigot at each camping area, and a campground host provides an added sense of security. The side road has the only bathrooms in the campground, but who's complaining—the campground is free. Campers can get a site almost anytime of year. A few weeks in March–April

CAMPGROUND RATINGS

Beauty:	★★★★
Site privacy:	★★★★
Site spaciousness:	★★★
Quiet:	★★★★
Security:	★★★★★
Cleanliness/upkeep:	★★★★★

The Natchez Trace Parkway is lined with interesting history, and a free campground.

WESTERN

and October–November—when snowbirds from up north are heading to and from their winter destinations—are the only times the campground is full. Otherwise, Meriwether Lewis is the domain of tenters during summer and fall.

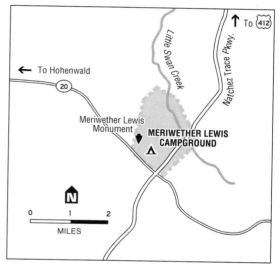

The Natchez Trace developed when boatmen, returning from delivering crops and other goods down the Cumberland, Ohio, and Mississippi rivers, used a buffalo and Indian path running from Natchez, Mississippi to Nashville, Tennessee to get back to their homes. As more people used this trail, the federal government commissioned roadwork, improving the path. The Natchez Trace became one of the United State's first western roads. Portions of this old road are actually preserved to this day and can be walked on. You'll have to learn the rest of the story on your own.

Some of my favorite sights along the parkway include the Gordon House, built in 1812; a preserved relic of an old tobacco farm, located just down the road from the Gordon House; and Jackson Falls, which exhibits some of the natural beauty of the region. This two-tiered fall drops over a rock rim and can be reached by trail. There are many more places to visit north and south of Meriwether Lewis Monument.

Near the campground is the actual monument to Meriwether Lewis, who, with William Clark, led the famous Corps of Discovery expedition up the Missouri River and overland to the Pacific in the early 1800s. After the expedition, Lewis died here under circumstances that remain one of the great mysteries in American history. He is buried at the monument.

Several miles of trails run along the ridges and hollows of the immediate area. Get a trail map at the log cabin near the monument. A longer hike lies north of here on the Natchez Trace National Scenic Trail. It runs for 26 miles in the vicinity of the Gordon House, north of the campground. Check out the picnic area at Little Swan Creek, an attractive stream with little bluffs running alongside its clear waters. A bigger waterway is the Buffalo River. It flows undammed for 110 miles past large bluffs that look over good fishing waters. Some of my most memorable paddling trips have taken place here. Fish for smallmouth bass or bream. Or just enjoy the scenery. Call (800) 339-5596 for an outfitter in nearby Hohenwald.

KEY INFORMATION

Meriwether Lewis Monument
2680 Natchez Trace Parkway
Tupelo, MS 38801

Operated by: National Park Service

Information: (800) 305-7417. www.nps.gov/natr

Open: Year-round

Individual sites: 32

Each site has: Picnic table, fire ring

Site assignment: First come, first served; no reservation

Registration: No registration

Facilities: Water spigot, flush toilets

Parking: At campsites only

Fee: No fee

Elevation: 900 feet

Restrictions:

Pets—On 6-foot leash only

Fires—In fire rings only

Alcoholic beverages—At campsites only

Vehicles—None

Other—14-day stay limit

To get there: From Columbia, take TN 50 west for 15 miles to the Natchez Trace Parkway. Head south on the parkway for 22 miles to Meriwether Lewis Monument, which will be on your right.

NATCHEZ TRACE STATE PARK AND FOREST

Lexington

The Natchez Trace was an old travel-and-trade route used by Indians and settlers. A western branch of this path that once connected Nashville, Tennessee and Natchez, Mississippi passes through this park, where today visitors hike, fish, swim, ride horses, and camp. The 48,000 acres of this attractive state park and forest had been among the most abused land in the state. Subsequent conservation, which begun in the 1930s, has rendered the Natchez an inviting destination. Miles of trails traverse woodlands, fields, streams, and shorelines, opening up many possibilities for hikers, mountain bikers, and equestrians.

The best destination for tent campers is Camping Area 1, located along a narrow ridgeline beside Cub Creek Lake. Twenty-three campsites are spread along both sides of a narrow ridgeline. Landscaping timbers have been used to level the campsites. Overhead is an oak-hickory forest with a fairly thick understory. The sites are well spread apart, though a thin understory lessens campsite privacy. Pass the bathhouse and drop down to the lake to find some coveted waterfront sites. Don't let the fact that these sites have water and electricity make you think this is an RV domain—the state park has built a new RV campground several miles away and all the big rigs head there. At the end of the gravel road is a small play area and a trail

CAMPGROUND RATINGS

Beauty:	★★★
Site privacy:	★★★
Site spaciousness:	★★★
Quiet:	★★★★★
Security:	★★★★
Cleanliness/upkeep:	★★★★★

The range of settings and activities are wide enough to suit the most diversely minded tent campers.

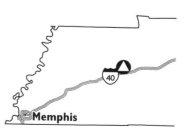

21

WESTERN

leading to the long foot-bridge crossing Cub Lake.

Camping Area 2 is near the lake, but not on the lake. It has been designated a wilderness camping area. Located up a hollow alongside two small streams, the 44 campsites have not been landscaped or leveled, giving them a more primitive appearance. The first few campsites lie below the confluence of these small streams and may get extra wet during a major storm. Grass forms the main understory beneath tulip

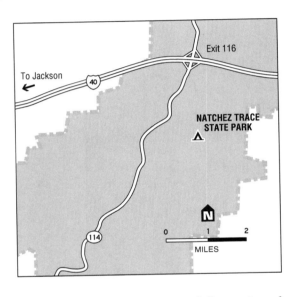

trees, sweetgums, ironwood, dogwoods, and oaks. Come to a fully equipped bathhouse and the campground road splits. The road to the right heads up the hollow of a small feeder stream. The sites are even hillier here, so be careful where you pitch your tent. The road ends in a tear drop–shaped loop with some widely separated sites.

The other campground road continues up the main hollow and splits left up a dry ridge. There are some sloped sites here, too. Top out by some nice sites, then dip back down into the main hollow. Here are a few sites that have electricity; they are also a bit larger than the others. Again, no RVs will dare drive up here. Water spigots are spread throughout the camping area. Beside the RV campground, Pin Oak, there is also a wrangler campground exclusively for folks with horses. Supplies are available at a park store open on weekends.

Recreation is easy here. Cub Lake has a swim beach, and rowboats and pedal boats are available for rent. If you seek the wilder side of Natchez, hit the Cub Creek Trail or the Deer Trail, located near the campground. The Fairview Gullies Trail will give you an idea of how far this area has come since it was once worn-out subsistence farmland a century ago. The Red Leaves Trail makes two loops big enough for overnight backpackers. If you want to ply the woods in an easier fashion, take a forest drive. The wildlife area has miles of marked gravel roads. Get a map at the park visitor center. Mountain bikers will need this map, too. Horseback trail rides can be undertaken at the stables near the wrangler camp.

Want to wet a line? Anglers can seek out any of the four lakes that dot the park. Cub Lake is 58 acres and just steps from your tent. Pin Oak Lake, Maple Lake, and Browns Creek Lake all offer angling for crappie, bluegill, bass, and catfish. Check out recreation equipment for many activities, such as croquet, badminton, and archery. There are more developed facilities here, but Natchez is spread out enough to where all park visitors can enjoy the recreation of their choice without detracting from the natural beauty of the area. Come see for yourself.

To get there: From Jackson, head east on I-40, to exit 116. Turn south on TN 114 and immediately enter the park.

KEY INFORMATION

Natchez Trace State Park and Forest
24845 Natchez Trace Road
Wildersville, TN 38388

Operated by: Tennessee State Parks

Information: (731) 968-3742; www.tnstateparks.com

Open: Camping Area 1, year-round; Camping Area 2, late May–mid-November

Individual sites: 7

Each site has: Camping Area 1, water, electricity, picnic table, lantern post, upright grill; Camping Area 2, picnic table, lantern post, upright grill, some fire rings

Site assignment: First come, first served; no reservation

Registration: Ranger will come by and register you

Facilities: Hot showers, water spigots

Parking: At campsites only

Fee: Camping Area 1, $17 per night; Camping Area 2, $6.50 nonelectric, $10 electric

Elevation: 400 feet

Restrictions:

Pets—On 6-foot leash only

Fires—In fire rings only

Alcoholic beverages—Not allowed

Vehicles—None

Other—14-day stay limit

NATHAN BEDFORD FORREST STATE PARK

Camden

The site of a Civil War engagement, the highest point in West Tennessee, attractive campsites right on Kentucky Lake . . . Nathan Bedford Forrest State Park is a park of superlatives. I'll admit it, this place far exceeded my expectations. When I arrived, I drove down to the Rustic Campground first and was happily surprised at the campsites. After I visited Pilot Knob's eye-popping view and learned the area's place in Tennessee history, the state park's fate was sealed—it was set for inclusion in this book.

Let's start with the Rustic Campground. Drive on a dead-end road to come alongside the dammed Tennessee River, now known as Kentucky Lake. Come to a small loop with a spur road heading to several campsites. The sites are large, level squares supported with landscaping timbers. Gravel pads keep the sites well drained. The lake is close enough to kick gravel into the water. A low railing keeps campers from falling off the platforms into the water or the ground below. A tall army of sweetgum trees shades the campsites, with a few dogwoods thrown in. A shoreline of small rocks makes entering the water easy. The water spigot is a short walk from the five sites.

Pass the boat ramp and come to the second loop. All the campsites here are lakeside as well. Campsites 10 and 11 share the same extra-large pad, so it could be used

CAMPGROUND RATINGS

Beauty:	★★★★★
Site privacy:	★★★
Site spaciousness:	★★★
Quiet:	★★★★
Security:	★★★★★
Cleanliness/upkeep:	★★★★★

The lakeside sites here will lure you back time and again.

WESTERN

as a double site. The loop ends at the site 13. Up the hill is a bathroom with flush toilets, and a water spigot is nearby. At the end of the road are two lesser-developed sites with picnic tables only.

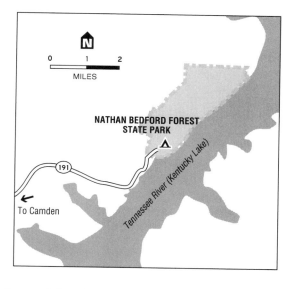

The Happy Hollow Campground is a 38-site affair located away from the lake. It is laid out in a classic loop up a small valley. The first few sites are a bit close together, resting beneath tulip trees, sweetgum, and oak. As the loop climbs a small hill, the sites become more appealing to sun lovers. Some of the sites and the fully equipped bathhouse are in the center of the loop. The sites become more spread out as you continue around the loop, but a minimal understory keeps campsite privacy about average. Drop back down to a streamside environment to some level, larger, and more attractive sites. A campground host is located here for your safety.

Anglers and boaters love the proximity of Kentucky Lake. You can almost fish from your tent at some of the sites at the Rustic Campground. There is no designated swim area, but a whole lake lies in front of you. However, before you hit the water, consider heading up to Pilot Knob. Grab a view from the point that rivermen used as a beacon for many a year. There is an interpretive center up here, too, that focuses on the life and times of those who used to live on the Tennessee River. Admire the memorial to Nathan Bedford Forrest and learn about the Civil War Battle of Johnsonville, where for the first time in history,= a cavalry force defeated a naval force. A ranger conducts programs during the warm season. Across the river, Johnsonville State Historic Area offers more insight into the battle and trails to explore the now-abandoned townsite.

The rugged beauty of the riverside terrain is revealed in the parks trail system, which covers over 25 miles of ground. Grab a map at the park office. Swing along Pilot Knob Ridge and drop down into hollows that lead to the river's edge. Or just cruise right along the river. Either way, you will be appreciative of the riverside beauty of this quality state park.

To get there: From the courthouse square in Camden, take TN 191 north for 8 miles to the state park.

KEY INFORMATION

Nathan Bedford Forrest State Park
1825 Pilot Knob Road
Eva, TN 38333

Operated by: Tennessee State Parks

Information: (731) 584-6356, www.tnstateparks.com

Open: Year-round

Individual sites: 15 nonelectric, 38 electric

Each site has: Rustic Camping has picnic table, upright grill; Happy Hollow has water, electricity, picnic table, upright grill

Site assignment: First come, first served; no reservation

Registration: Ranger will come by and register you

Facilities: Flush toilets, water spigots; Happy Hollow has hot showers

Parking: At campsites only

Fee: $3 entrance fee; Rustic Campground, $10 per night; Happy Hollow tents, $14 per night; RVs, $17 per night

Elevation: Rustic Campground, 360 feet; Happy Hollow, 460 feet

Restrictions:

Pets—On 6-foot leash only

Fires—In fire rings only

Alcoholic beverages—Not allowed

Vehicles—None

Other—14-day stay limit

PICKWICK LANDING STATE PARK

Savannah

Pickwick Landing State Park has a dizzying array of offerings, many of which don't necessarily appeal to tent campers, like a lodge and golf course. However, it also has features that do lure our kind, like the 75-site tent campground located in Bruton Branch Recreation Area. A lot of lake separates the 350-acre Bruton Branch from the balance of the state park, which has the lodge and another, more developed campground. Nearby, outside the park, is the site of one of the most notorious battlefields in the United States— Shiloh. Absorbing the history of this major Civil War conflict was certainly a worthwhile day in my life. Come to Pickwick; stay at Bruton Branch and tour Shiloh National Military Park while you are here.

In all fairness, tent campers need to hear about the main campground. The electric and water hookups spell RV, but many of the paved pull-ins are so sloped no self-respecting big-rig driver would park there, unless they like sleeping on a hill. However, leveled camping areas fix that problem, so tent campers can enjoy this area. The wooded campground is spread out in a series of small, interconnected loops beneath thick hickory-oak-pine woods. The campsites are well spaced and separated by trees. Full-service bathhouses serve the area.

Across the Tennessee River, which is dammed at this point and known as Pick-

CAMPGROUND RATINGS

Beauty:	★★★★
Site privacy:	★★★
Site spaciousness:	★★★
Quiet:	★★★
Security:	★★★★
Cleanliness/upkeep:	★★★★

Camp at Bruton Branch Recreation Area and tour Shiloh Battlefield while you are here.

WESTERN

wick Lake, lies Bruton Branch Recreation Area. Bruton Branch is divided into numbered areas. Area 1 and Area 2 are situated in a cove of the lake. These sites are wooded, with a grassy understory and are well spaced, but a lack of understory minimizes campsite privacy, though this allows good lake views. Many of the sites are directly lakeside. Area 1 and Area 2 have 13 sites altogether. Continue down Bruton Branch Road and pass a few day-use areas. The final 62 campsites

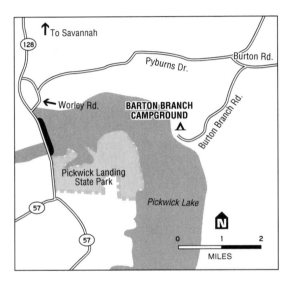

start again with Area 5 through Area 8. The cove has now given way to the main lake, and the lakeside sites have far reaching views down to Pickwick Dam and across the lake to the main park. Just past Area 5 the campground begins to widen and sites are located away from the lake as well as on it. Young hardwoods shade most of the sites.

A swim beach and boat landing break up the camping area. Farther down the campground widens again into three rows of campsites. All the campsites have a view of the lake, but the direct lakeside sites offer first-rate views and water access. A fully equipped bathhouse stands beside a small ranger station. There is a water spigot here, too. The campground narrows again beyond the bathhouse, then ends along with the dead end of Bruton Branch Road.

Swimming, fishing, and boating are the top activities at Bruton Branch. Visitors can rent boats across the lake, at the main park, and two more swim beaches are located here should a change of scenery be desired.

Also at the main park are volleyball, badminton, and other field games. There is also a hiking trail, but if you want to walk around I suggest you make the short drive to Shiloh National Military Park.

First go to the Shiloh visitor center and look around, maybe take in the video presentation. Cars or bikes (bring your own) can take the historical tour route. Pull over and walk around to see the sights here. It will give you a real insight into the Civil War—you will learn of strategies undertaken by Gen. U.S. Grant and Gen. Albert Sidney Johnston (the highest-ranking American officer ever killed in battle) and how the Union vessels on the nearby Tennessee River influenced the outcome of this two-day clash. See the memorials to the soldiers of various states who fought here. Then get a close-up view of the dark side of war at the infamous Bloody Pond and learn about how Shiloh was the first place where military field hospitals were used. Beyond the main tour route, historic old roads and trails beg further exploration. The sobriety of Shiloh will help you appreciate the pleasantries of your life as you enjoy Bruton Branch.

To get there: From the junction with US 64 in Savannah, head south on TN 128 for 9.8 miles to Worley Road. Turn left on Worley Road and follow it for 0.5 mile to Pyburns Drive. Turn right on Pyburns Drive and follow it 5 miles to Bruton Road. Turn right on Bruton Road and follow it for 0.5 mile to Bruton Branch Road. Veer right on Bruton Branch Road and follow it to a dead end at the recreation area. The main campground is down TN 128 just beyond Pickwick Dam.

KEY INFORMATION

Pickwick Landing State Park
P.O. Box 15
Pickwick Dam, TN 38365

Operated by: Tennessee State Parks

Information: (731) 689-3129; www.tnstateparks.com

Open: Mid-March through mid-October

Individual sites: 123

Each site has: Bruton Branch has picnic table, fire ring; Main Campground has water, electricity, picnic tables, upright grill, fire ring

Site assignment: First come, first served; no reservation

Registration: Ranger will come by and register you

Facilities: Hot showers, water spigots, pay phone, ice machine

Parking: At campsites only

Fee: Bruton Branch $8 per night; Main Campground $14 per night for tents, $17 per night for RVs

Elevation: 420 feet

Restrictions:

Pets—On 6-foot leash only

Fires—In fire rings only

Alcoholic beverages—Not allowed

Vehicles—Maximum 2 vehicles per site

Other—14-day stay limit

MIDDLE TENNESSEE

BLEDSOE CREEK STATE PARK

Gallatin

Bledsoe Creek is a wooded refuge from the ever-escalating pace in Nashville. Life was far different two hundred years ago. At Bledsoe Creek State Park, you can explore what it was like back then while enjoying the modern recreation of this state park set on the shores of Old Hickory Lake. The campground is a real hit-and-miss affair—a hodge-podge of good and not-so-good campsites—though discriminating campers will find a site to suit their needs. I recommend inspecting the entire campground before picking your site. The campground fills only on summer holiday weekends, but get here early on other weekends so you can get one of the better sites.

The campground is situated on a hilly peninsula, surrounded on three sides by Old Hickory Lake. Enter the campground and come to Deer Run Road. This section of the campground is open year-round. The road swings around toward the lake. The campsites have paved pull-ins, some of which have little level ground for a tent. There are several larger lakeside sites. A dock lies at the end of the road. The understory is mostly grassy with some brush.

Continuing along the main park road, Woodchuck Hollow is the next campground road you reach. There is a real mixture of sun and shade, with some vegetation between the campsites and oaks and cedars being the dominant trees.

CAMPGROUND RATINGS

Beauty:	★★★
Site privacy:	★★★★
Site spaciousness:	★★★★
Quiet:	★★★
Security:	★★★★★
Cleanliness/upkeep:	★★✧★★

Bledsoe Creek makes a quick getaway from Nashville and is close to some interesting Tennessee history.

MIDDLE

Many campsites have circular picnic tables. The latter half of the loop has large sites. This camping area, like the others, has a bathhouse.

You'll reach Blue Heron Drive area next. The heavily shaded lakefront sites here are the best ones in the park. The best of the best are on the auto turnaround at the end of the loop. These sites will go first. Some sites are pull-up, others pull-through. The last area is Rabbit Jump Hill, which has widely separated sites. Some are shady and some aren't. What

makes it unusual is a pond at the center of the auto turnaround. The sites along Main Park Road (sites 103–114) do not have water or electricity and are favored by tent campers. Some are good, but some are too sloped for a good night's sleep. Be discriminating when you pick a site.

Once you have chosen your site, hit the water or hit the trails. A boat ramp at the campground makes pleasure boating easy. You can fish Old Hickory or ski. Most anglers go for crappie, bluegill, bass, and catfish. Boatless fishermen can use the campground fishing dock.

This state park is managed as an environmental education area. Your tickets to learning about the state park are the four miles of trails easily reached from the campground. Check out the lake along the Shoreline Trail, then get the view from up top on the High Ridge Trail. Combine the two for a good loop hike. There are shorter trails, too, including the Birdsong Interpretive Nature Trail.

If you like a taste of history, you might head up the road to Cragfont, the preserved home of General James Winchester. He was a hero of the Revolutionary War and the War of 1812. The fine stone and woodwork of this 1802 house will impress. You can also enjoy views of the garden and the surrounding area, as Cragfont was built high on a bluff. Also nearby is Wynnewood, set near mineral springs that attracted buffalo in days before the United States existed. This two-story log inn was built by A.R. Wynne as a stagecoach stopover and getaway for those enjoying the springs. This National Historic Landmark survived the Civil War and is furnished with items of its era. Wynnewood is east of the state park on TN 25. To the west of the park, in Hendersonville, is Rock Castle, the limestone and wood home of Daniel Smith, a Revolutionary War officer. For detailed information on these historic sites, contact the park office. A trip here is worth it—just pick a good site and you will have a good time.

To get there: From downtown Gallatin, head east TN 25 for 5 miles to Zieglers Fort Road. Turn right on Zieglers Fort Road and follow it 1.8 miles to the park entrance, on the left.

KEY INFORMATION

Bledsoe Creek State Park
400 Zieglers Fort Road
Gallatin, TN 37066

Operated by: Tennessee State Parks

Information: (615) 452-3706; www.tnstateparks.com

Open: Deer Run open year-round; rest of campground mid-April–November

Individual sites: 114

Each site has: Picnic table, rock fire ring; most have water and electricity

Site assignment: First come, first served; no reservation

Registration: Self-registration on-site

Facilities: Hot showers, flush toilets, pay phone, laundry

Parking: At campsites only

Fee: $10 per night tent sites, $17 water and electricity sites, $19 waterfront sites

Elevation: 500 feet

Restrictions:

Pets—On 6-foot leash only

Fires—In fire rings only

Alcoholic beverages—Not allowed

Vehicles—None

Other—14-day stay limit

CEDARS OF LEBANON STATE PARK

Lebanon

Cedars of Lebanon State Park doubles as a recreation getaway and a preserve for a unique remnant of cedar forest native to Tennessee. As nearby Nashville grows, these 9,000 acres will become even more valuable. Tent campers will value this campground as it separates tents, pop-ups and vans from RV campers. Developed recreation, such as a pool and game courts, lie near the campground, allowing campers to enjoy these amenities and also explore the cedar forests that brought about the preservation of this area in the first place.

Not surprisingly, the campground is in a cedar forest. The first area, campground 1, is laid out like a parking lot, with pull through sites and way too much paving. This is the RV headquarters, so don't even bother looking. Campground 2 has no restrictions but is primarily enjoyed by tent campers. It is much more heavily wooded and has a lot less paving. Campsites lie on both sides of the loop, which has a little vertical variation and some hardwood trees. Some sites are little close together, but will do. Gravel pads ringed by landscaping timbers make it more conducive for tent campers. The best site in the park is campground 3. It is the largest in size, yet has the fewest campsites, meaning more campsite privacy and spaciousness. Grass and brush form the understory beneath a forest that thickens beyond the first few campsites. The paved

CAMPGROUND RATINGS

Beauty:	★★★★
Site privacy:	★★★★
Site spaciousness:	★★★
Quiet:	★★★★
Security:	★★★★
Cleanliness/upkeep:	★★★★

This state park has America's largest remaining cedar forest and more.

MIDDLE

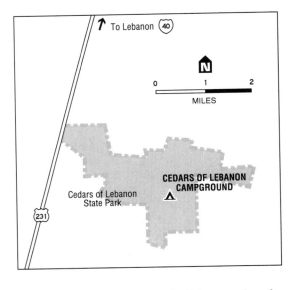

To Lebanon (40)

N

0   1   2
MILES

CEDARS OF LEBANON
CAMPGROUND

Cedars of Lebanon
State Park

(231)

pull-ins do not diminish the atmosphere here. The campsites in the back half of the loop are very spread apart and are raised a bit, as heavy rains can inundate the woods near the loop. An intermittent streambed runs along side the far end of the loop. The last few sites are open and sunny, which are desirable on cooler days. Each loop has its own bathhouse and water spigots.

A camp store and laundry, open during the warm season, is accessible to all campers. Campsites at Cedars of Lebanon are readily available, save for summer holiday weekends. Also readily available are many camper activities. An ultra large swimming pool is just a short walk from the campground, as is a disc golf course. You can purchase a disc at the camp store. The swimming pool is open Memorial Day to Labor Day. Game courts are an activity option, whether you choose volleyball, horseshoes or tennis.

If you are looking for more interpretive activities, head for the park nature center, which is open during summer. Interpretive programs teach kids and adults about insects, snakes and how nature works. They will also tell you about the cedar glades of the area. These cedar glades are natural clearings in the forest that host such plants as cactus, reindeer moss and other living things unusual for this region. The cedar trees, for which the park is named, were used by early settlers for cabins, fences and roof shingles. This wood was desirable since cedar split easily and was rot resistant. Later, the cedar forests were commercially logged. The harvested wood was primarily used in pencil making, as its wood is light and easily sharpened. Today, this cedar forest has made a comeback and can be seen along the 8 miles of park trails that wind through the evergreens. Other shorter nature trails, such as the Limestone Sinks Trail and the Hidden Springs Trail are good leg-stretchers. If you don't feel like walking, you can go horseback riding. A park stable offers guided rides through the Middle Tennessee woods along miles of bridle paths. After coming here, you will be appreciative of this remnant forest so accessible from the capital of Tennessee.

To get there: From exit 238 on I-40 near Lebanon, head south on US 231 for 6 miles to the state park entrance, which will be on your left.

KEY INFORMATION

Cedars of Lebanon State Park
328 Cedar Forest Road
Lebanon, TN 37090

Operated by: Tennessee State Parks

Information: (615) 443-2769, www.tnstateparks.com

Open: Year-round

Individual sites: 117

Each site has: Picnic table, fire ring, water and electricity, lantern post, upright grill

Site assignment: First come, first served; no reservation

Registration: At campstore in summer, ranger will come by in winter

Facilities: Hot showers, flush toilets, pay phone

Parking: At campsites only

Fee: $3 entrance fee; tent, $14 per night; RV, $17 per night

Elevation: 700 feet

Restrictions:

Pets—On 6-foot leash only

Fires—In fire rings only

Alcoholic beverages—Not allowed

Vehicles—None

Other—14-day stay limit

FALL CREEK FALLS STATE PARK

Pikeville

It is only fitting that Fall Creek Falls—considered by many to be not only Tennessee's best state park, but one of the finest in the Southeast—would have some of the best walk-in tent campsites around. Of course, this 20,000-acre preserve is more widely known for its natural features: verdant old-growth forests, rock outcroppings, and sandstone bluffs overlooking steep gorges, and of course clear streams that fall to circular pools that give this park atop the Cumberland Plateau its name. Within this park are activities galore—if you can't do it here, you probably can't do it outside either.

What about these terrific walk-in tent sites? They have been a fairly recent addition to the park. It's a great thing for tent campers, too, because the main campground doesn't even begin to reach the high standards of beauty set by the tent sites. Suffice it to say that the maze of overcrowded sites situated among too many loops doesn't make for a pleasant camping experience. Sure, some decent sites are tucked away in the main campground, but with those walk-in tent sites available, I wouldn't bother. On the plus side, some of the primary sites can be reserved, but that only testifies to the busyness of the main campground. Sometimes it seems like you are in a small city-of-the-woods. Keep in mind that the above campground ratings describe the walk-in sites only.

CAMPGROUND RATINGS

Beauty:	★★★★★
Site privacy:	★★★★★
Site spaciousness:	★★★★★
Quiet:	★★★★
Security:	★★★★
Cleanliness/upkeep:	★★★

Fall Creek Falls is widely considered Tennessee's premier state park.

MIDDLE

The path to the walk-in sites starts behind the E Loop bathhouse. The trail immediately splits. The right trail heads past the only close walk-in site, then dips down a hollow. It then reaches a flat in a pine-oak forest with a well-groomed site off to the right. Drop down toward another hollow and come to two more sites that are so widely separated that campers at one can't see the other. The farthest site is about 150 yards from the road. The left-hand trail leads to farther camp-

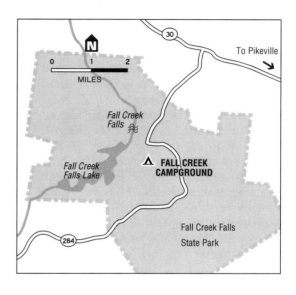

sites. Drop down to a fern hollow, then climb a hill. Here is the first of five sites so far apart you begin to wonder if the sites are really out here. They are, and they are good. Walk-in campers use the E Loop bathhouse. During my mid-week, mid-summer stay, the main campground was nearly full, while only one of the nine walk-in sites was occupied. Walk-in tent sites cannot be reserved. On weekends, water- and electricity-loving campers will take walk-in sites out of desperation. Barring summer holidays, you can get a walk-in site during the week and on Friday during summer weekends. Getting a site is easy during shoulder seasons. I recommend coming during fall colors.

What should you do first? Start by heading to the Nature Center. Inside are displays about the park. Get a trail map and visit the falls. Cross Cane Fork on a swinging bridge above a cascade. The pool below this cascade serves as a summertime swimming hole. (The park does have a regulation swimming pool.) Take the Gorge Trail to observe Cane Creek Falls, then check out gorge overlooks before coming to Fall Creek Falls. You can curve around and walk to the base of this 256-foot drop. Longer trails include the nearby Paw-Paw

Trail and two long loops for overnight backpackers. Fall Creek Lake makes a pretty impoundment in the upper Fall Creek valley. Rent canoes, pedal boats or johnboats. No gas motors are allowed on here, but fishing is, and it's reputed to be good.

If you don't feel like walking, ride a bike. Rental bikes are available at Village Green Area, where a recreation hall, visitors lounge, and park information center stand. Take a trail ride at the park stables. For cars, the one-way Gorge Scenic Drive circles around the edge of the Cane Creek Gorge, then up Piney Creek Gorge where you can check out Piney Creek Falls. Park naturalists conduct nature programs; kids ages 12 and under have their own programs. Take a pontoon boat ride, tour Camp's Branch Cave, or go on a group bike ride. Ball courts are available for tennis, softball, and basketball. If you don't feel like cooking, grab a meal at the park restaurant, where they have breakfast, lunch, and dinner buffets. Come to think of it, a trip to Fall Creek Falls could be called an outdoor buffet.

To get there: From Pikeville, head west on TN 30 for 12 miles to TN 284. Turn left on TN 284 and keep forward for a little over 4 miles to reach the campers registration booth. The walk-in tent sites are nearby.

KEY INFORMATION

Fall Creek Falls State Park
Route 3, Box 300
Pikeville, TN 37367

Operated by: Tennessee State Parks

Information: (423) 881-3297; reservations (800) 250-8611

Open: Year-round

Individual sites: 9 walk-in tent sites, 228 others

Each site has: Walk-in sites have picnic table, fire ring, lantern post, tent pad; others have water and electricity

Site assignment: Walk-in sites are first come, first served; some others can be reserved

Registration: At camper registration station

Facilities: Hot showers, flush toilets, water spigots, laundry, pay phone, camp store

Parking: At walk-in parking area and at campsites

Fee: $10 per night walk-in tent sites; $17 per night other

Elevation: 1,700 feet

Restrictions:

Pets—On 6-foot leash only

Fires—In fire rings only

Alcoholic beverages—Not allowed

Vehicles—None

Other—14-day stay limit

HENRY HORTON STATE PARK

Chapel Hill

Henry Horton is classified as a state resort park, which means it has a golf course, lodge, cabins, and more. However, for tent campers and outdoor recreation enthusiasts, Henry Horton has another side—two tent-camping areas and the beauty of the Duck River. This appealing canoeing stream flows through heart of the park, in between massive rock bluffs and tree-lined banks. The Duck also serves as a division between the resort side of the park and the more rustic part that appeals to tent campers. So pitch your tent and then head down the Duck for a fun Middle Tennessee float trip.

The fairly large campground here has two areas for tent campers—the tent area and the wilderness area. Using the word "wilderness" is stretching it a bit, but this nine-site area is nevertheless ideal for tent campers. Set apart from the rest of the campground, the wilderness area has its own side road, which straddles the border between a field on one side and dense woods on the other. The ground is level beneath the forest of oak, hickory, and cedar. Smaller trees such as dogwood form a dense understory, and the many rock outcrops add to the scenic beauty of the campsites. The campsites are large and well spaced from one another as they stretch out along the gravel road. There is a small auto turnaround at the end of the road.

CAMPGROUND RATINGS

Beauty:	★★★
Site privacy:	★★★★★
Site spaciousness:	★★★★
Quiet:	★★★
Security:	★★★★★
Cleanliness/upkeep:	★★★★

The Wilderness Camp adds to the appeal of this park on the banks of the Duck River.

MIDDLE

A second area for tent campers lies near the Duck River at the beginning of the main campground. These nine sites are laid out on a gravel road with a small spur road near one of the bathhouses. The whole area dips toward the Duck River. The campsites are shady here, but they don't have the dense understory that the Wilderness Camp has. This understory here is grassier.

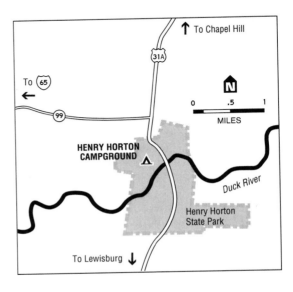

The main campground is laid out in a large paved loop. The loop heads clockwise in a shady woodland. There are pull-in and pull-through sites on slightly hilly terrain. A campground host enhances campground security. The sites become more pinched in toward the end of the loop. Overall, this is the land of RVs and should be left to them. I recommend the wilderness sites over all the rest. They are near-ideal sites for tent campers, and they are also the cheapest. If you decide to visit, keep in mind that the park fills on summer holiday weekends and during occasional nearby special events.

Named after the 36th governor of Tennessee, the land for this park was donated by the Wilhoite family, into which ol' Henry Horton married. It offers a little bit of everything for visitors. Here is a quick rundown of available activities: tennis, badminton, basketball, disc golf, volleyball, and a skeet shooting range. The resort has an Olympic-sized pool with lifeguards on duty in summer. On the more rustic side is the Turkey Trail, which makes a 2.5-mile loop. The Wilhoite Mill Trail, where Henry's relatives ground their meal, courses alongside the Duck River past machine relics from days gone by. Small side trails lead to bluffs overlooking the Duck River and to swimming and fishing access points. The shorter Hickory Ridge Nature Loop starts near the wilderness camping area. It connects to the park nature center, where a park recreation director, on duty during the summer months, has all sorts of activities for kids and adults alike, from horseback riding to hay rides. Call ahead for a weekly list of activities.

Many folks come to Henry Horton not only to camp but also to float the Duck River. A nearby outfitter makes this pastime convenient for those who don't have their own canoe or who are looking for a shuttle. Duck River Canoe Rental at Forest Landing is just north of the park on US 31A. They offer a fine day-trip from Hopkins Bridge to end at the state park. Choose a canoe or sea kayak and float-fish for bass or beam, take a dip in the water, or just enjoy the riverside sights. For a reservation, call the outfitter at (931) 364-7874.

To get there: From exit 46 on I-65 near Columbia, head east on TN 99 for 13 miles to US 31A. Turn right on 31A and follow it for 2 miles south to the state park, which will be on your right.

KEY INFORMATION

Henry Horton State Park
P.O. Box 128
Chapel Hill, TN 37034

Operated by: Tennessee State Parks

Information: (931) 364-2222, www.tnstateparks.com

Open: Year-round

Individual sites: 9 tent sites, 9 wilderness tent sites, 54 RV sites

Each site has: Wilderness Camp and Tent Camp have picnic table, fire grate; rest of campground has picnic table, upright grill, fire grate, water, electricity

Site assignment: First come, first served; no reservation

Registration: Campground host will register you

Facilities: Hot showers, flush toilets, pay phone

Parking: At campsites only

Fee: $10 per night tent sites, $6.50 per night wilderness sites, $17 per night RV sites

Elevation: 600 feet

Restrictions:

Pets—On 6-foot leash only

Fires—In fire rings only

Alcoholic beverages—Not allowed

Vehicles—Maximum 2 vehicles per site

Other—14-day stay limit

MONTGOMERY BELL STATE PARK

Dickson

Montgomery Bell was a Middle Tennessee mover and shaker back in the early 1800s. He moved to Dickson County to work the burgeoning iron ore industry. Some of the ore Bell actually extracted was used in cannonballs by Andrew Jackson in the Battle of New Orleans in 1812. Bell recognized the natural beauty of the area beyond the economic appeal, as did later Tennesseans, who established this state park. Today, you can enjoy the popular campground, hiking trails, and more that comprise this state park.

The campground is large and well laid out in a flat along the banks of Hall Creek. Pass the camper check-in station and turn right onto the main loop. This begins the area of tent sites. A tall cedar and hardwood forest shades the camping area. The tent sites in the center of the loop are in a park-like setting. The area is very level and the sites are spacious, but the grassy understory minimizes campsite privacy. Some sites on the outside of the loop are a little too sloped for a good night's sleep. A crossroad with more tent sites bisects the main loop, which swings around toward Hall Creek. All the sites are alluring save for a few more hillside ones. The main loop then comes alongside Hall Creek and the end of the tent sites. However, the campsites along Hall Creek are available to tent campers. These sites are fairly large and offer access to the clear stream overly-

CAMPGROUND RATINGS

Beauty:	★★★
Site privacy:	★★★
Site spaciousness:	★★★★
Quiet:	★★★★
Security:	★★★★★
Cleanliness/upkeep:	★★★★★

This popular campground is convenient to Nashville.

MIDDLE

ing flat slabs of limestone. A bluff stands across the creek.

Sites continue along both sides of the main campground loop. The farther upstream along the creek, the more RVs are in evidence. Beyond the main loop is one more loop that is wide open to the sun with campsites that are too close together; avoid these. Three bathhouses are spread along the campground. Tent campers should seek out sites 51 through 104.

Montgomery Bell's proximity to Nashville makes it a

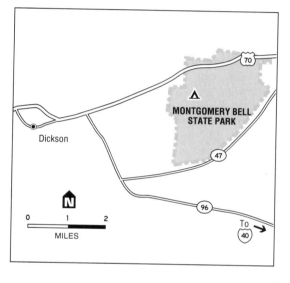

convenient getaway for city residents, but it also fills the campground on summer holidays and other warm-weather weekends. Try to get here early on Friday if you can. Better yet, come during the week. Our visit was on a warm summer weekday, and the campground had a sleepy feel to it. Hall Creek was flowing lazily to meet Jones Creek. We could have taken a nap but instead made a hiking loop out of the campground using a combination of trails. Even though it was mid-afternoon, we came upon a deer and fawn, which were stirring despite the heat. The deer surprised us as we dipped into a hollow and continued on enjoying the shady woods. Later we had a picnic in lower Wildcat Hollow, discussing what else we could do here. And there is plenty.

Lake Acorn has a swim beach to cool off after a hike like ours. If you love to be on the water but not in it, try a canoe, rowboat, or paddleboat. Many folks like to fish this lake for catfish, bream, and bass. If Lake Acorn isn't producing, try the other park lakes, Woodhaven and Creech Hollow.

Game players can try croquet, shuffleboard, volleyball, and tennis. Nature enthusiasts can enjoy the park's trail system. The master trail is the Montgomery Bell Trail, which makes an 11.5-mile loop through the park. A cross trail, Creech Hollow, makes five-mile loop hikes possible on the Montgomery Bell Trail. Shorter paths include the Ore Pit Trail, which examines the mining history of the park, and the J. Bailey Trail that makes a loop near the park headquarters. Campers will use the Wildcat Trail to leave the campground to connect to the Montgomery Bell Trail and others. In summer, park naturalists are on hand to give campfire programs and nature presentations, as well as more kid-oriented activities such as arts and crafts. I can't say for sure, but I believe Montgomery Bell would be proud of his eponymous state park.

KEY INFORMATION

Montgomery Bell State Park
P.O. Box 39
Burns, TN 37029

Operated by: Tennessee State Parks

Information: (615) 797-9052, www.tnstateparks.com

Open: Year-round

Individual sites: 27 tent sites; 94 water and electric sites

Each site has: Picnic table, fire ring

Site assignment: First come, first served; no reservation

Registration: At campground registration hut

Facilities: Hot showers, flush toilets

Parking: At campsites only

Fee: $3 entrance fee; $11 per night tent site, $17 per night water and electric sites

Elevation: 650 feet

Restrictions:

Pets—On 6-foot leash only

Fires—In fire rings only

Alcoholic beverages—Not allowed

Vehicles—Maximum 2 vehicles per site

Other—14-day stay limit

To get there: From exit 182 on I-40, head west on TN 96 for 11 miles to US 70. Turn right on US 70, then head 4 miles east to the state park entrance, which will be on the right.

46

MOUSETAIL LANDING STATE PARK

Parsons

Mousetail Landing. What a name! As odd a name it may be, here's the story of its origin. A tannery was built on this site back in the early 1800s. The many fresh animal skins awaiting the tanning process attracted mice. No one knew how many until a fire broke out. All at once, mice by the thousands tore out of the tannery and rushed to the river landing, which then became known as Mousetail Landing. Don't worry, the mice are gone. Instead there is a great state park with two good but different campgrounds to pitch your tents and enjoy the finer things a park has to offer, like swimming, fishing, boating, and backwoods hiking.

The Primitive Campground is the tenter's choice. Located on the Spring Creek embayment of the Tennessee River, the camping area is shaded by a forest of shagbark hickory, sweetgum, winged elm, and various oaks. The first two campsites are isolated from the other sites. Beyond here the campground road passes over a wet weather drainage to enter a super shady flat with large campsites. The road turns right. Several waterside camps with a grassy understory spur off the main road. The sites then become more spacious and heavily shaded. The main channel of the Tennessee River comes into view. A few open sites stand near the river. Directly beside the Tennessee is a picnic area and grassy lawn with a few trees interspersed.

CAMPGROUND RATINGS

Beauty:	★★★★
Site privacy:	★★★
Site spaciousness:	★★★★
Quiet:	★★★★
Security:	★★★★
Cleanliness/upkeep:	★★★★★

Both waterside and hilltop sites await you by the Tennessee River.

MIDDLE

Here, campers can watch the tugboats pass by as they push barges up and down the mighty river.

The Main Campground is in the park proper, a mile or so from the Primitive Campground. Located high on a wooded ridge, the 25 sites are spread out on three mini-loops. The first loop is for tenters only and has no water or electricity. A mixture of grass and trees make it more open. The hillside drops off steeply from the edge of the campsites that have been leveled with landscaping timbers. Tent pads have been installed, too. Pass the modern bathhouse and come to the next loop. These sites have water and electricity. Hickories shade the camping area. The third loop has 10 sites and is more shaded. The small dead-end side road has a few desirable sites. Vegetation has been added wherever the sites lacked privacy.

I stayed in the Primitive Campground on my visit. Spring was breaking loose, and it seemed the trees were greening before my very eyes. Late in the evening I walked out to the water and watched the sun set as a barge chugged around the bend. Most folks bring their own boats during the warmer months, pulling them right up to the riverside sites. Swimming is allowed but is at your own risk. There is a swim beach at the main park. Fishing is popular year-round for catfish, bass and bream.

Back on land, the Day Use Trail makes a three-mile loop from the park office down toward the river and up Sparks Ridge. This trail can also be accessed by a spur trail from near the campground. Hardier hikers will want to tackle the Eagle Point Loop. It runs up Kelly Hollow, over Sparks Ridge, and down to

Parrish Branch to near the original Mousetail Landing. From here, it ascends a bluff to a great view. It then skirts along the Lick Creek embayment before climbing a steep hill, completing the eight-mile loop. Just outside the park is another hike to a great view from Lady Finger Bluff. This is a Tennessee Valley Authority Small Wild Area. A trail map and directions are available at the park office. Start on the far side of the Lick Creek embayment and make a three mile cruise to a rock outcrop framed in gnarled, old red cedar trees that offers a sweeping view of the Tennessee River. Whether from Lady Finger Bluff or the Primitive Campground, you will come to view this slice of the Volunteer State as a good place to be.

> **To get there:** From Parsons, drive east on US 412 for 10 miles to TN 438. Turn left and follow TN 438 east for 2.1 miles to the state park, on your left.

KEY INFORMATION

**Mousetail Landing State Park
Route 3, Box 280B
Linden, TN 37096**

Operated by: Tennessee State Parks

Information: (731) 847-0841; www.tnstateparks.com

Open: Year-round

Individual sites: 46

Each site has: Primitive Area has picnic table, lantern post, upright grill, fire ring; Main Area has water, electricity, picnic table, upright grill

Site assignment: First come, first served; no reservation

Registration: Ranger will come by and register you

Facilities: Hot showers, water spigots at Main Area; vault toilets at Primitive Area

Parking: At campsites only

Fee: Primitive Campground $6.50 per night; Main Campground $10 per night non-electric sites, $14 per night electric sites

Elevation: Primitive Campground 360 feet; Main Campground 580 feet

Restrictions:

Pets—On 6-foot leash only

Fires—In fire rings only

Alcoholic beverages—Not allowed

Vehicles—Maximum 2 tents per site

Other—14-day stay limit

OLD STONE FORT STATE ARCHEOLOGICAL PARK

Manchester

This state archeological park preserves a 2,000-year-old American Indian ceremonial site on a 50-acre swath between the Little Duck and Duck rivers. The exact purpose of this area, enclosed by earth and stone walls that connect to bluffs of the rivers, may never be known. But it can be hypothesized that the Indians appreciated the beauty of this area as much as we can today. In what is now the state park, the two rivers drop off Highland Rim Plateau into the Nashville Basin, pouring forth their waters over big falls beside steep bluffs, which then meet at the south end of the park. Trails course through the area and along the wall of the ceremonial site. The topper is a cool, shady campground on the banks of the Duck River that makes an ideal retreat when the dog days of summer hit.

Enter the state park, then cross the narrow bridge over the Duck River to reach the campground entrance station. You'll find yourself in a very dense deciduous forest with a thick understory. Three loops spur off the main campground road, but the pretty forest is so dense it makes the 51-site camping area seem very intimate. Paved campsite pull-ins spur off the main campground road. The thick understory of brush and small trees offers the maximum in campsite privacy, which is further enhanced by well-separated campsites. The ground is mostly level and in places

CAMPGROUND RATINGS

Beauty:	★★★★
Site privacy:	★★★★★
Site spaciousness:	★★★★
Quiet:	★★★★
Security:	★★★
Cleanliness/upkeep:	★★★★

The tableland between the Duck and Little Duck rivers has been regarded as special for thousands of years.

MIDDLE

may be prone to ponding after a big storm. Each of the three loops heads toward the Duck River. Some sites on each loop have obscured views of the watercourse as it flows toward Bluehole Falls, which is audible from the lower part of the campground. Two modern bathhouses serve the three loops.

Even though all the campsites have hookups, the campground does not resemble an RV dealership. The Old Stone Fort attracts many families and campers of all stripes. Tenters dominate the scene in summer, and RVs have a stronger presence in the cooler months, though the campground as a whole is quiet in winter. The Old Stone Fort fills only on summer weekend holidays, and with the cool, deep woods, it never gets an overcrowded feel no matter the time of year.

The Old Stone Fort was never a fort in a defensive sense. Early Tennessee settlers gave it that name. Archeologists have determined that the walls delineated a ceremonial site—an enclosure built and rebuilt over a 400-year period from 30 AD to 430 AD. River cliffs were used as part of the wall system. At the entrance to the Old Stone Fort is a museum, which offers insight into the daily life of the Indians who built the structure. Ranger-led programs are offered on summer weekends. Look over the exhibits inside, then tour the site for yourself. The Wall Trail makes a 1.3-mile loop along the walls and cliffs that encircle the 50-acre ceremonial site. Smaller side paths lead past the three major falls of the park. Bluehole Falls and Big Falls are on the Duck River and Step Falls is on the Little Duck River, adding natural beauty to the historic setting. These rivers also offer fishing for bream and bass.

In later days, settlers saw the falls as a source of power, and many dams were built (and sometimes washed away) to provide energy for saw mills, paper mills, and grist mills. Today, one dam still stands on the Duck River above Blue Hole Falls, accessible via a trail from the campground. Another short nature trail loops through the woods from a trailhead near the campground entrance station. Other, wilder trails in the park include the Backbone, Little Duck Loop, and Old River Channel trails. These all spur off the Wall Trail and work through the tableland between the confluence of the two rivers. The confluence of history, beauty, and quality camping makes the Old Stone Fort a "no brainer" for tent campers interested in exploring Tennessee.

To get there: From exit 111 on I-24 near Manchester, take TN 55 west for one mile to US 41. Turn right and head north on US 41 through Manchester for 2 miles to Old Stone Fort Archeological State Park, which will be on your left.

KEY INFORMATION

Old Stone Fort State Archeological Park
Route 7, Box 7400
Manchester, TN 37355

Operated by: Tennessee State Parks

Information: (931) 723-5073, www.tnstateparks.com

Open: Year-round

Individual sites: 51

Each site has: Picnic table, fire ring, water, electricity, upright grill

Site assignment: First come, first served; no reservation

Registration: Ranger will come by and register you

Facilities: Hot showers, pay phone

Parking: At campsites only

Fee: $3 entrance fee; tents, $14 per night; RVs, $17 per night

Elevation: 1,000 feet

Restrictions:

Pets—On 6-foot leash only

Fires—In fire rings only

Alcoholic beverages—Not allowed

Vehicles—None

Other—14-day stay limit

PINEY

Dover

Three-hundred-eighty-four can be a scary number. At least when you are talking about the number of campsites in a campground. This usually spells an over-crowded city of RVs, with congestion, mayhem and all the things from which you are trying to get away. Piney, however, defies these expectations. This getaway on the south side of Land Between the Lakes has two loops catering to tent campers and a third loop that offers a good electrical option. The campground is well run. Add in the recreation opportunities—boating, hiking, fishing, and historical study— and you have a quality destination that tent campers can enjoy.

There are a total of eight loops in the campground, but tent campers only need be concerned about three of them. Dismiss Chestnut, Shortleaf, Dogwood, Persimmon, and Loblolly loops. The tents used at these loops are square, metal, have wheels, and have TV antennas sticking out of them. For tent campers who like electricity, head to the Black Oak Loop, located to the right after the campground entrance. Pop-up campers and such will be found here, but so will tent campers. This area is situated on a peninsula jutting into Kentucky Lake and has 92 campsites spread out along three loops. Thirty or so sites enjoy lake frontage, where campers pull up their boats. Some of this frontage is on a small lake cove, as opposed to the main lake. A

CAMPGROUND RATINGS

Beauty: ★★★★
Site privacy: ★★★
Site spaciousness: ★★★★
Quiet: ★★★★
Security: ★★★★★
Cleanliness/upkeep: ★★★★★

Don't let the size of this place scare you. Two good loops cater to tent campers.

MIDDLE

hickory and oak woodland shades the widely separated sites. The large campsites have been leveled, but the scant understory decreases campsite privacy. Small, wet weather drainages break up the terrain. A grassy area lies between the camping area and a swimming beach. One of the two bathhouses has showers.

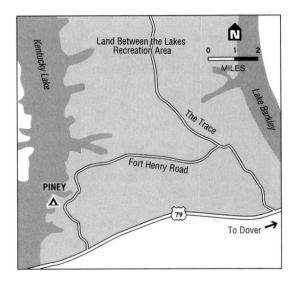

The other two loops of interest, the Virginia and Sweetgum loops, do not have electricity and thus are the realm of tent campers. To reach these, head left from the entrance to the 34-site Sweetgum loop, shaded by sweetgum, oaks, and cedars. A couple of small crossing roads have campsites. Most sites at the beginning are inside the loop, then you swing by the lake and come to some fine sites overlooking the water about 30 feet away. The end of the loop has some decent sites that are a little close together. The Virginia Loop has 23 sites shaded by pines and oaks. The loop descends toward the water. Six waterside sites are some of the best in the entire campground. Other sites here are a little too cramped for my taste. The end of the loop has ultra-shady sites good for a hot summer afternoon.

Water spigots are strategically situated throughout the loops, and here a fully equipped bathhouse serves both loops. Locals are the primary tent campers, which is a good sign, since they don't just happen on this camp-ground. Piney generally fills on summer holiday weekends. Other than that, you should have no trouble getting a site. An on-site store offers most camp-ing supplies.

Now, what to do? The campground roads are great for biking, and bikes are available for rent at the camp store. Better yet, bring your own two-wheeler. Go boating in Kentucky Lake. Or fish. Or fish without a boat at Catfish Pond. Or dip yourself in the water at the swim beach. Hikers have the Fort Henry trail system to tackle. There are 26 miles of paths here, and you can actually trace Gen. U.S. Grant's movements between Fort Henry and nearby Fort Donelson. These forts were the sites of the first Civil War attacks on the river routes of what was then part of the American West. A Fort Henry Trail map reveals numerous loop possibilities. The Piney Trail leads from near the campground into this trail network.

Fort Donelson, just a few miles away on the Cumberland River, is a national battlefield and where the star of U.S. Grant first rose. You can tour the battlefield by walking seven miles of interpretive trails or by auto. Check out the river battery's big guns and the still-standing Dover Hotel, where the losing side surrendered. At Piney Campground you won't surrender to boredom or crowds, just to the acceptance of a good tent-camping destination.

To get there: From Dover, head west on US 79 for 12 miles to Fort Henry Road. Turn right on Fort Henry Road and follow it 2.3 miles to the campground, which will be on your left.

KEY INFORMATION

Piney
100 Van Morgan Drive
Golden Pond, KY 42211

Operated by: United States Forest Service

Information: (270) 924-2000, www.lbl.org

Open: March–November

Individual sites: 384

Each site has: Virginia and Sweetgum loops have picnic table, fire grate, lantern post; Black Oak Loop has electricity, picnic table, fire grate

Site assignment: First come, first served; no reservation

Registration: At campground kiosk

Facilities: Hot showers, water spigots, pay telephone, camp store

Parking: At campsites only

Fee: $12 per night spring and fall; $3 per night electricity at Black Oak Loop; $13 per night during summer

Elevation: 360 feet

Restrictions:

Pets—On 6-foot leash only

Fires—In fire rings only

Alcoholic beverages—At campsites only

Vehicles—1 wheeled camping vehicle per site

Other—21-day stay-limit

ROCK ISLAND STATE PARK

McMinnville

These days, the hand of man is often seen as a destructive force in nature. Here at Rock Island State Park, human forces unintentionally created what many Tennesseans (the author included) consider to be the state's prettiest waterfall. IHere's the story. In 1915, Tennessee Electric Power Company dammed the Caney Fork River. This dam backed up the Caney Fork and the nearby Collins River, creating Great Falls Lake. This raising of the water level forced water from the Collins River through caves that emerged on a rock face of the Caney Fork River. Since then, and to this day, water courses through the caves, then makes a 300-foot-wide, 80-foot drop over a rock bluff into the Caney Fork River. This drop is known as Twin Falls. Great Falls, the lake's namesake, is actually a different scenic cascade within the park boundaries. This watery beauty is only part of the picture, however. A tent-only camping loop, trails, swim beaches, and more make Rock Island State Park a great destination.

Let's start with the campground. Pass the park office and turn left into the tent loop. The gravel road passes beside a fully equipped bathhouse, then enters shady woods of pine and cedar. This shade keeps the understory minimal. The campsites are average in size and are evenly spaced from one another. Even though this is a designated tenter's loop, each site has water

CAMPGROUND RATINGS

Beauty:	★★★★
Site privacy:	★★★
Site spaciousness:	★★★
Quiet:	★★★
Security:	★★★★★
Cleanliness/upkeep:	★★★★★

Rock Island packs an enormous amount of beauty into its boundaries.

MIDDLE

and electricity. Some campsites are stretched out along
the auto turnaround. These
are the biggest and best
sites.

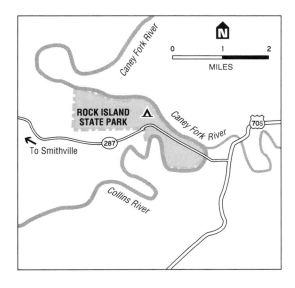

The main campground
has a trading post and hosts
both tent and RV campers.
Steep bluffs drop off the
edges of the camping area.
Paved pull-ins beneath the
pines and mixed hardwoods
attract RVs. The last part of
the campground, starting
with site 31, is more conducive to tent campers.
Here, the sites are spread far
apart on the outside of the
road, overlooking wooded drop-offs. The forest is thicker, creating more
campsite privacy. Two bathhouses, a pavilion, and a playground serve the
main campground. Tent campers will want to try the tent loop first, then this
camping area. Rock Island fills only on summer holiday weekends, so getting
a site is not often a problem—though campsite reservations are available,
unlike at most Tennessee state parks.

Everybody loves to visit the falls here. Twin Falls Overlook is on the far side
of the Caney Fork River from the campground. Cross the Great Falls Dam on
the way to the overlook. Many canoers and kayakers use the Sand Bar Launch
Ramp to paddle to Twin Falls, which look enormous from the bottom. Mother
Nature didn't need any help with the swimming facilities at Rock Island. A
natural sand beach is located just below the boat ramp. Swimmers enjoy the
cool waters of the Caney Fork River while taking in the setting—clear, green
waters backed by a tall rock bluff that makes any man-made swimming pool
look paltry. Others rock-hop and swim below Great Falls. Trails are another
way to see the park. The Collins River Nature Trail makes a loop in the land

between the Collins and Caney Fork Rivers. The Eagle Trail leaves directly from Badger Flats and leads down to the banks of the Caney Fork. There is even a short mountain-bike trail.

Rock Island State Park borders the uppermost reaches of Center Hill Lake. Boaters can take off from the park to explore the lake and fish, or they can use the boat ramp on the lower Collins River and try their luck there. Game players can use the tennis, basketball, and volleyball courts, after checking out equipment free of charge at the ranger station. The rangers at Rock Island pride themselves on their nature programs. There is a full-time park naturalist and an extra naturalist on staff in summer. Woods walks, cave trips, canoe trips, bird walks, and more keep the kids busy and help adults learn more about the beauty here, whether it is totally natural or got a little help from man.

KEY INFORMATION

Rock Island State Park
82 Beach Road
Rock Island, TN 38581

Operated by: Tennessee State Parks

Information: (931) 686-2471, www.tnstateparks.com

Open: Year-round

Individual sites: 60

Each site has: Picnic table, fire ring, water, electricity, upright grills

Site assignment: First come, first served and by reservation

Registration: At campground check-in station

Facilities: Hot showers, flush toilets, telephone

Parking: At campsites only

Fee: Tent $11 per night; RV $16 per night

Elevation: 950 feet

Restrictions:

Pets—On 6-foot leash only

Fires—In fire rings only

Alcoholic beverages—Not allowed

Vehicles—None

Other—14-day stay limit

To get there: From Smithville, at the junction with US 70, take TN 56 south for 9.5 miles to TN 287. Turn left on TN 287 north and drive 10.5 miles to the state park entrance, which will be on your left.

RUSHING CREEK

Dover

I have enjoyed Rushing Creek in spring, summer and fall. Suffice it to say you can't go wrong here. Spring offers the promise of renewal, as the plants and animals come to life. Summer is the setting for water fun on Kentucky Lake. Fall is the time to enjoy the land-based recreation opportunities, like hiking. Other nearby attractions can be enjoyed no matter the season. Rushing Creek campground exudes the aura of an old-time camp; it has a relaxed feel, yet there is plenty to do in the area.

Let's start with the campground. Drop down to the shores of Kentucky Lake and come to the pay station. A campground host is situated nearby, from March through October, for your safety and convenience. Keep forward and follow a gravel road toward the lake, passing a bathhouse with showers. To the left is a large picnic shelter in a grassy waterside field. To the right are three shady sites beneath oak trees. These sites feature awesome lake views. Back up to the pay station and a loop heads to the right, up a small hollow. Oaks, hickories, cedar, and sycamore trees shade these 12 average-sized campsites that have a grassy understory. Several sites are secluded by distance. The final site has electricity, and it is the only one in the campground that does. A water spigot lies near this electric site.

CAMPGROUND RATINGS

Beauty: ★★★★
Site privacy: ★★★★
Site spaciousness: ★★★★
Quiet: ★★★★
Security: ★★★★
Cleanliness/upkeep: ★★★★★

The name doesn't do this relaxing campground justice.

MIDDLE

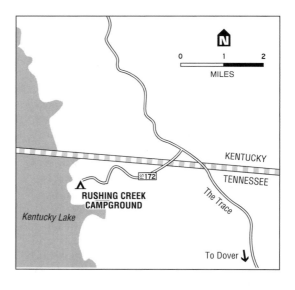

Another road leaves left from the pay station, up the hollow of an intermittent stream to well-shaded sites. Two small bridges span the stream beside a small field. The loop road rises slightly, but the sites have been leveled with landscaping timbers. Two other sites lie along a dead-end road and are so far from the others you won't be able to see another camper unless you set out to do so.

Also nearby is Jones Creek Camping Area. You passed the turn for it just before reaching Rushing Creek. To reach Jones Creek, backtrack to the signed turn and follow a gravel road down to a flat beside Kentucky Lake. Fourteen campsites (unnumbered but with picnic tables and fire rings) are spread along an intermittent streambed. A picnic shelter stands on a hill nearby; it's equipped with a vault toilet and has no water, but it offers the maximum in solitude. A boat ramp lies near the camping area. Rushing Creek will only fill on summer holiday weekends; summer weekends in general are the most crowded. Solitude is guaranteed in winter. The bathhouse showers are closed from November through February.

Most recreation is centered on Kentucky Lake. Boaters can launch from the camp ramp. Others will be seen fishing from shore or swimming in the cove that opens to the main body of the lake. A playground with basketball goals and badminton nets is located near the campground host. The field adjacent to the lake beckons a kite to be flown or ball to be tossed. It can function as a place for kids to run around while the adults relax at camp.

If you want to roam with a purpose, take the Walker Line Trail to the North-

South Trail, which stretches for 68 miles, running the length of Land Between the Lakes. You can walk or drive to the Homeplace–1850. This is a working 19th-century farm where interpreters in period clothing demonstrate the daily lives of settlers from the 1850s. On this farm are 16 original and restored structures from the Land Between the Lakes area. Just across the road from the Homeplace–1850 is the Buffalo Range and Trail. Here, buffalo live on a fenced range. You can see them as they live out their lives in this section of Tennessee as they once did long ago. North of Rushing Creek, just over the Kentucky state line, is the Golden Pond Visitor Center and Planetarium. It has programs that look to the heavens and offers public star observation sessions. Also nearby is the Elk & Bison Prairie. This is a restored "barren," a habitat once favored by elk and buffalo. You can take an auto tour of this wildlife-rich locale. Actually, the whole of Land Between the Lakes is rich with outdoor opportunities of all kinds.

To get there: From Dover, head south on US 79 for 5 miles to access the Trace. Turn right on the Trace and drive 16.5 miles north to Forest Road 172 and follow it to dead-end at the campground.

KEY INFORMATION

Rushing Creek
100 Van Morgan Drive
Golden Pond, KY 42211

Operated by: United States Forest Service

Information: (270) 924-2000; www.lbl.org

Open: Year-round

Individual sites: 40

Each site has: Picnic table, fire grate

Site assignment: First come, first served; no reservation

Registration: Register with host March–October; November–February, self-registration on site

Facilities: Hot showers, water spigots March–October; vault toilets November–February

Parking: At campsites only

Fee: $9 per night March–October; $8 per night November–February

Elevation: 360 feet

Restrictions:

Pets—On 6-foot leash only

Fires—In fire rings only

Alcoholic beverages—At campsites only

Vehicles—15-mph campground speed limit

Other—21-day stay limit

EASTERN
TENNESSEE

BANDY CREEK CAMPGROUND

Oneida

The National Park Service is catching on quite nicely. It realizes there are two divergent groups that use campgrounds: tent campers and RVers. Here at Bandy Creek Campground, the Park Service has designated a tents-only loop that places compatible groups together. It's a good thing because a recommended campground completes the superlative outdoor package that is the Big South Fork.

Protected since 1974, the Big South Fork features wild rivers, steep gorges, thick forests, and human history set atop the Cumberland Plateau. A well-developed trail system departs directly from the campground, making an exploration of the Big South Fork easy. There are also opportunities for mountain biking, canoeing, fishing, and rafting.

Bandy Creek Campground is a large complex with a total of four camping loops. A recreation area and the park's Visitor Center are nearby. Loop A is the only loop exclusively available to tent campers. It veers off to the left after the campground registration booth and is separated from the rest of the campground.

The campground is generally wooded. A few sites back up against a field and the recreation complex, which includes a swimming pool and a playground for young campers. Since Bandy Creek is on the plateau, the forest is mixed hardwood with oaks, tulip trees, and Virginia pine.

CAMPGROUND RATINGS

Beauty:	★★★
Site privacy:	★★★
Site spaciousness:	★★★★
Quiet:	★★★
Security:	★★★★
Cleanliness/upkeep:	★★★★★

Bandy Creek Campground lies at the heart of the 100,000-acre Big South Fork National River and Recreation Area.

64

EASTERN

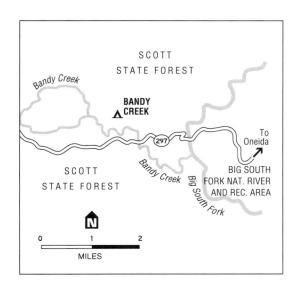

The campsites themselves are mostly open, bordered by a dense woodland.

A mini-loop extends off Loop A and contains four out-of-the-way sites. Beyond the first mini-loop, campsites with paved parking areas extend on either side of the road as it rises slightly, passing one of the two most complete washhouses I've ever encountered. The buildings are designed to resemble local architecture and have a water fountain, piped water, flush toilets, showers, and even a two-basin sink for washing dishes! Farther on, the road divides and arrives at one of two bad sites in the campground: site 32 is adjacent to the water tower, and site 2 backs against the swimming pool.

As Loop A swings around, another mini-loop veers off. It contains seven wooded sites that are the most private in the campground. The main road passes the second washhouse. Three other water pumps are dispersed among the 49 well-kept sites.

The rest of the campground contains 96 sites. Only Loop D, with 52 sites, is open to both tents and RVs during the winter. The pool is open from June to Labor Day, but the rest of this place is ready to be explored year-round.

Hiking is very popular. Why not? Trails lace the immediate area. The John Litton/General Slavens Loop traverses six miles of the surrounding countryside. It descends to the valley where the John Litton Farm stands, passes a large rock house, and climbs back up to the campground via Fall Branch Falls. If you prefer a trail with more human and natural history, take the Oscar Blevins Loop. It is a moderate, 3.6-mile loop that passes the Blevins Farm, some large trees, and more of the steep bluffs that characterize the Cumberland Plateau. Another hiking option is the easy Bandy Creek Campground loop. It is a short, 1.3-mile family hike that offers a good introduction to the area. Want more trails? Stop by the Visitor Center, and they can point you in the right direction.

If you don't feel like walking, ride a horse. The nearby Bandy Creek Stables offer guided rides for a fee.

Water enthusiasts should drive the short distance to Leatherwood Ford and the Big South Fork for recreation. There the river flows through a scenic gorge with steep cliffs soaring to the sky. Exciting rapids and decent fishing can be found both upstream and down. Check the Visitor Center for river conditions. I have used and recommend Sheltowee Trace Outfitters for boat and shuttle service. Their phone number is (800) 541-RAFT. Mountain biking is also big in the Big South Fork. Again, check with the Visitor Center for the best of many trails that crisscross the park.

It is evident you won't be spending much time relaxing at the campground. There is simply too much to see and do. Come see the Big South Fork and you'll have spent your time well.

To get there, from Oneida take TN 297 west for 14 miles. Bandy Creek Campground will be on your right.

KEY INFORMATION

**Bandy Creek Campground
Route 3, Box 401
Oneida, TN 37841**

Operated by: National Park Service

Information: (931) 879-4869 or (800) 879-4869; www.nps.gov/biso

Open: April–October; limited sites year-round

Individual sites: 49, tents only

Each site has: Tent pad, fire grate, picnic table, lantern post

Site assignment: By reservation or first come, first served

Registration: Self-registration on site; reserve by phone, (800) 356-2267, or online, reservations.nps.gov

Facilities: Water, flush toilets, hot showers, pay phone, swimming pool

Parking: At campsites only

Fee: $15 per night; $18 with water

Elevation: 1,500 feet

Restrictions:

Pets—On a 6-foot or shorter leash

Fires—In fire grates only

Alcoholic beverages—At campsites only

Vehicles—Maximum 2 vehicles per site

Other—14-day stay limit

CARDENS BLUFF

Hampton

If Cardens Bluff were private land it would go for big, big bucks. The scenery is that outstanding. Luckily for us tent campers, we can overnight here for ten bucks a shot. Tall mountains rise from the clear blue-green water of Watauga Lake. The camping area stands on a peninsula jutting into the dammed Watauga River. To make a good thing even better, the forest service has improved the campground by revamping old sites and adding walk-in tent sites and a new bathhouse with showers. To make a good thing even better, Watauga Lake offers a swim beach, boat ramp, and hiking trails that meander through the nearby Pond Mountain Wilderness. However, Cardens Bluff is such an appealing campground that you may not even want to leave your site.

Exit TN 67 and enter the campground. A few sites are along the road before it makes a loop. Pass the campground host and a bathroom. Begin a series of sites that are cut into the hillside of the wooded bluff. Very few sites are directly beside the road. The dense forest screens the sites from one another and provides good shade for summer days. Soon you'll reach the main bathhouse, a Forest Service state-of-the-art model. The wood building has individual bathrooms for each gender with sinks and showers. Below you to the left are several of the newest walk-in tent sites, each with a picnic table, fire ring, lantern post, tent

CAMPGROUND RATINGS

Beauty:	★★★★★
Site privacy:	★★★★
Site spaciousness:	★★★
Quiet:	★★★
Security:	★★★★
Cleanliness/upkeep:	★★★★

A recent facelift improved this ideally located campground on Watauga Lake.

EASTERN

pad, and a covered food preparation table with two levels, one of which is ideal for cooking while standing. These five sites offer a mixture of sun and shade.

Just past here is an exit road with one campsite (site 12). This offers the maximum in solitude. Another road leads to a hilltop knob with five sites perched there. The main campground road curves around the peninsula and comes to a group of seven sites on a mini-peninsula of their own. They are cut into the bluff and offer

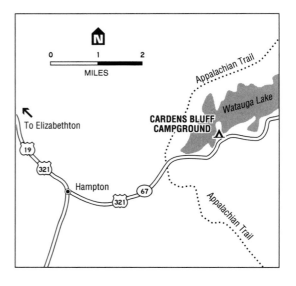

great lake views. Keep swinging around the hillside to reach sites situated on both sides of the steep hill. Attractive rockwork and site leveling enhances the camps. Farther along the main loop are more roadside sites. Look for a trail leaving right that heads to four first-rate walk-in tent sites that even the most discriminating tent camper would love. Of special note is site 42, which commands a view of the lake. Having such a great campground will make it more desirable and thus busier. Nice summer weekends will fill the place, so get here early if you can. You can find a site most any weekday save for summer holidays. There is only one shower-equipped bathhouse, but four other bathrooms are spread through the campground, as are water spigots.

At nearly 2,000 feet, Watauga Lake stays invigoratingly cool, even in the dead of summer. The Watauga River drains the high country of upper East Tennessee and North Carolina. This clear mountain water makes for an ultraclear lake. Just down the way is the Rat Branch boat ramp, where you can get your craft in the water and have a ball, whether you are fishing or just boating. Also down the lake is the Shooks Branch Recreation Area, which has a swim beach. Maybe they put the swim beach here for the Appalachian Trail thru-hikers since the AT runs right by. If you leave south from Shook Branch on the AT, enter the Pond Mountain Wilderness and climb to Pond Flats four miles distant. If you head north, the AT skirts around the lake to reach Watauga Dam in three miles. The northbound hiking is easier. The Cardens Bluff Trail is also easy. It leaves near campsite 12 and circles around the shoreline. If you want a tough climb, head up the Pond Mountain Trail. This path makes a 3.3-mile climb of Pond Mountain to a point known as Bear Stand, also in the wilderness. Pick up this trail 1.5 miles farther down TN 67 beyond the entrance to Carden Bluff. The Watauga Point Recreation Area is only a mile down TN 67. This spot also has a swim beach, picnic area, and a gravel path looping through the woods. This whole area is known as the Watauga Recreation Corridor, and as you can read, there is plenty going on here.

KEY INFORMATION

Cardens Bluff
4400 Unicoi Drive
Unicoi, TN 37692

Operated by: U.S. Forest Service

Information: (423) 638-4109; www.southernregion.fs.fed.us/cherokee

Open: Mid-April–mid-October

Individual sites: 43

Each site has: Picnic table, fire ring, lantern post, tent pad, some have additional cooking tables

Site assignment: First come, first served; no reservation

Registration: Self-registration on site

Facilities: Hot showers, flush toilets, water spigots

Parking: At campsites only

Fee: $10 per night

Elevation: 1,990 feet

Restrictions:

Pets—On 6-foot leash only

Fires—In fire rings only

Alcoholic beverages—At campsites only

Vehicles—Maximum two vehicles per site

Other—14-day stay limit

To get there: From the junction of US 19 and US 321 in Elizabethton, head south on US 321/US 19/TN 67 for 5 miles to Hampton. Here, TN 67 turns left into Hampton. Follow TN 67 East for 4.1 miles to the campground, on your left.

COSBY CAMPGROUND

Gatlinburg

Set on a slight incline in what once was pioneer farmland, this attractive, terraced campground is surrounded on three sides by mountains. The large camping area is situated between the confluence of Rock Creek and Cosby Creek. During my trips to the area, I have rarely seen Cosby Campground crowded, whereas other equally large Smokies campgrounds are sometimes cramped, noisy, and overflowing. Several loops expand the campground, and bathrooms are conveniently located throughout the site. A small store, specializing in campers' needs, is located at the turn off TN 32.

Now beautifully reforested, this area is rich in Smoky Mountain history. Cosby was one of the most heavily settled areas in the Smokies before Uncle Sam began buying up land for a national park in the East. The farmland was marginal anyway, so in order to supplement their income, Cosby residents set up moonshine stills in the remote hollows of this rugged country. As a result, Cosby became known as the "moonshine capital of the world."

In remote brush-choked hollows and along little streamlets, the "blockaders"—as moonshiners were known—established stills. Before too long they had clear whiskey ("mountain dew") ready for sale. Government agents, known as "revenuers" and determined to stop the production and sale of "corn likker," battled

CAMPGROUND RATINGS

Beauty:	★★★★★
Site privacy:	★★★★
Site spaciousness:	★★★★★
Quiet:	★★★★
Security:	★★★★
Cleanliness/upkeep:	★★★★★

Located off the principal tourist circuit, this cool, wooded campground makes an ideal base for exploring the virgin forests and high country of the Cosby/Greenbriar area.

EASTERN

the moonshiners through-out the hills. It is doubtful if any stills are operating with-in the park boundaries today; however, in other areas of Cocke County, someone is surely practicing the art of "feeding the fur-nace, stirring the mash, and judging the bead."

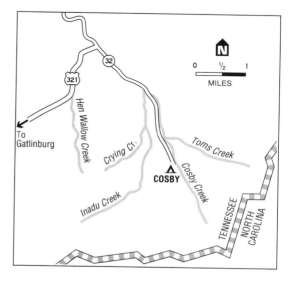

Its past is what makes Cosby so interesting. Trails split off in every direction, allowing campers to explore the human and natural his-tory of this area. Follow the Lower Mount Cammerer Trail for 1.5 miles to Sutton Ridge Overlook. On the way to the overlook, watch for signs of homesteaders from bygone days: rock walls, springs, and old chimneys. At the overlook, you'll get a good lay of the land: Gabes Mountain to your east, the main crest of the Smokies to your south, the Cosby Valley below, and East Tennessee on the horizon.

Another hiking option is the Gabes Mountain Trail. Along its 6.6-mile length, this trail passes picturesque Henwallow Falls and meanders through huge, old-growth hemlock and tulip trees and scattered, old homesites. Turn around at the Sugar Cove backcountry campsite.

Don't forget to explore nearby Greenbrier. The 4-mile Ramsay Cascades Trail traverses virgin forest and ends at a picturesque waterfall that showers hikers with a fine mist. The Brushy Mountain Trail winds its way through sev-eral vegetation zones to an impressive view of the looming mass of Mount LeConte above and Gatlinburg below. Grapeyard Ridge Trail is the area's most historical and secluded hike. Walk old country paths along Rhododen-dron Creek and count the homesites amid fields just now being obscured by the forest. At three miles, just before the Injun Creek backcountry campsite, look for the old tractor that made its last turn in these Smoky Mountains.

The crown jewel trail from Cosby Campground is the six-mile hike to the restored Mount Cammerer fire tower. Built on a rock outcrop, it was formerly called White Rock by Tennesseans and Sharp Top by Carolinians. It has since been renamed Mount Cammerer, after Arno B. Cammerer, former director of the National Park Service. Restored by a philanthropic outfit called Friends of the Smokies, the squat, wood-and-stone tower was originally built by the Civilian Conservation Corps during the Depression. The 360° view is well worth the climb. To the north is the Cosby Valley and the rock cut of I-40. Mount Sterling and its fire tower are to the south. The main crest of the Smokies stands to the west, and a wave of mountains fades off into the eastern horizon.

Cosby Campground is a real winner. In the summer, naturalist programs in the campground amphitheater offer campers a chance to learn more about the area from rangers and other park personnel. The campground's size allows campers to set up near or away from others to achieve their perfect degree of solitude. If you are in the mood for company, however, the tourist Mecca of Gatlinburg is nearby. There, you can visit an Elvis museum, see a musical revue, stock up on souvenirs, and stuff yourself with taffy.

To get there, from Gatlinburg take US 321 east until it comes to a T intersection with TN 32. Follow TN 32 a little over a mile, turning right into the signed Cosby section of the park. After 2.1 miles, arrive at the campground registration hut. The campground is just beyond the hut.

KEY INFORMATION

Cosby Campground
107 Park Headquarters Road
Gatlinburg, TN 37738

Operated by: Great Smoky Mountains National Park

Information: (865) 436-1200; www.nps.gov/grsm

Open: May–September

Individual sites: 175

Each site has: Picnic table, fire pit, lantern post

Site assignment: First come, first served; no reservations

Registration: At the hut at the campground's entrance

Facilities: Cold water, flush toilets

Parking: At individual sites

Fee: $14 per night

Elevation: 2,459 feet

Restrictions:

Pets—On leash only

Fires—In fire pits

Alcoholic beverages—At campsites only

Vehicles—None

Other—7-day stay limit during the summer

FOSTER FALLS RECREATION AREA

Tracy City

The south end of the Cumberland Plateau has some of the wildest, roughest country in Tennessee. Sheer bluffs border deep gulfs—what natives call gorges. In these gorges flow wild streams strewn with rock gardens hosting a variety of vegetation. Intermingled within this is a human history of logging and mining that has given way to the nonextractive use of nature: ecotourism.

Foster Falls Recreation Area is operated by the Tennessee Valley Authority. It offers a safe and appealing base for your camping experience in the South Cumberlands. The campground is situated on a level, wooded tract near Foster Falls. It features the classic loop design, only the loop is so large it seems to engulf the 26 sites spread along it. Hardwoods give way to pines as you head toward the forested back of the loop. An interesting tree in the campground is the umbrella magnolia. Its leaves can reach two feet in length, causing its limbs to sag during the summer. Look for the tree along the campground entrance road and among sites 1–10.

The spindly, second-growth tree trunks form a light understory, but the campsites are so diffused that site privacy isn't compromised. The understory actually lends a parklike atmosphere to the campground. Foster Falls has some of the most spacious campsites I've ever seen. The large, concrete picnic tables have concrete bases to

CAMPGROUND RATINGS

Beauty:	★★★
Site privacy:	★★★
Site spaciousness:	★★★★★
Quiet:	★★★
Security:	★★★★★
Cleanliness/upkeep:	★★★★

Foster Falls Recreation Area can be your headquarters for exploring the South Cumberland Recreation Area.

EASTERN

keep your feet clean during those rainy times. Tent pads are conspicuously absent, but there is plenty of flat terrain for pitching your tent.

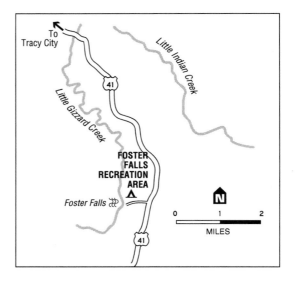

The three water spigots are handy to all campsites, but the comfort station is located on one side of the loop, making a midnight bathroom run a little long for those distant campers. However, this campground is rarely full, so you should be able to secure a site near the comfort station if you prefer a shorter trip. Quite often, your camping companions will be rock climbers, for Foster Falls has quietly emerged as the premier rock-climbing area in the Southeast.

A campground manager lives on site across from the campground entrance for your security (and your gear's) while you check out the rest of the South Cumberland Recreation Area. The SCRA has eight different units, totaling over 12,000 acres, ready for you to enjoy.

For starters, a connector trail leaves the campground to Foster Falls. Here, you can take the short loop trail that leads to the base of 120-foot falls, or you can intersect the south end of the Fiery Gizzard Trail and see Foster Falls from the top looking down. If you take the Fiery Gizzard Trail, you will be rewarded with views into Little Gizzard and Fiery Gizzard gulfs. Trail signs point out the rock bluffs where rock climbers ply their trade. The first 2.5 miles offer many vistas and small waterfalls where side creeks plunge into the gorge below. My favorite view is from the Laurel Creek Gorge Overlook, where rock bluffs on the left meld into forested drop-offs beyond, contrasting with the flat plateau in the background.

Other must-sees in the South Cumberlands are Grundy Forest, Grundy Lakes, Savage Gulf, and the Great Stone Door. Administrators at Foster Falls will direct you to all the sights.

Grundy Forest contains about four miles of the most feature-packed hiking you can ask for: waterfalls, rock houses, old trees, old mines, and strange rock formations. Just remember to watch where you walk, as the trails can be rough.

Grundy Lakes State Park is on the National Historic Register. Once the site of mining activity, this area has seen prison labor, revolts, and the cooling down of the infamous Lone Rock coke ovens. The Lone Rock Trail will lead you to all the interesting sites.

At Savage Gulf State Natural Area, three gorges converge to form a giant crow's foot. An extensive trail system connects the cliffs, waterfalls, sinkholes, and historic sites of the area. The Great Stone Door is a 10-by-100–foot crack in the Big Creek Gorge that was used by Indians who traversed Savage Gulf.

The campground at Foster Falls is pleasant enough to stay a week or more, and that's about how long you'll need to get a good taste of the South Cumberland Recreation Area.

To get there, from Tracy City take US 41 south for 8 miles and turn right at the sign for Foster Falls. The campground will be 0.3 mile on your left.

KEY INFORMATION

Foster Falls Recreation Area
498 Foster Road
Sequatchie, TN 37374

Operated by: Tennessee Valley Authority

Information: (423) 942-9987 or (800) 882-5263; www.tva.gov

Open: Early-April–mid-November

Individual sites: 26

Each site has: Fire grate, picnic table, lantern post

Site assignment: First come, first served; no reservations

Registration: Resident manager will come by to register you

Facilities: Water, flush toilets

Parking: At campsites only

Fee: $11 per night

Elevation: 1,750 feet

Restrictions:

Pets—On a 6-foot leash only

Fires—In fire grates only

Alcoholic beverages—Not allowed

Vehicles—None

Other—14-day stay limit

FRANKLIN STATE FOREST

South Pittsburgh

Located just south of Suwanee, Franklin State Forest is one of those quiet, out-of-the-way places that seems known only among local folks. However, word is spreading about this mountain biking and hiking Mecca, where the Cumberland Plateau drops sharply into Swedens Cove, forming an escarpment where the views span the trail system that runs along its edge. Tent campers will find the campground here quite rustic, even down to the homemade picnic tables. The Tennessee Division of Forestry will be the first to tell you they aren't in the campground business. However, they do maintain this pretty little camp beside a small lake for those who want to explore the 7,000-acre slice of plateau country near the Alabama border.

To reach the camping area, drive down gravel Lake Road and you'll soon come to a solo campsite on the right-hand side near TN 156—perfect for those who seek maximum solitude. The site rests in a grassy area ringed in trees with a little gravel turnaround. Drive farther down the road to reach the main camping area, situated in a hickory-oak forest beside the spring-fed pond. Three separate campsites are spread along the waters, near an earthen dam. The homemade picnic tables, which add a neat rustic touch, are made from small trunks of trees topped with rough-cut lumber. The sites are plenty spacious, and privacy is really not much of an issue, as this

CAMPGROUND RATINGS

Beauty:	★★★★
Site privacy:	★★★
Site spaciousness:	★★★★
Quiet:	★★★★★
Security:	★★★
Cleanliness/upkeep:	★★★

It's designation as a state forest keeps Franklin little-used, though its natural beauty exceeds that of many state parks.

EASTERN

campground is rarely used during weekdays, nor is it much crowded on weekends. Continue on the gravel road below the dam and drive through the lake outflow to reach the rest of the camping area, located on the far side of the lake. There is a large campsite here along with a rough wood privy.

Bought from a coal operation in 1936, the forest was developed by the Civilian Conservation Corps into what you see today. Miles of old roads cover the forest, beckoning exploration by foot, bike, or car.

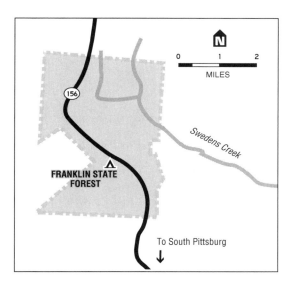

The entire trail system is accessible from the campground. Pump up the tires on your mountain bike and head for the rim of the Cumberland Plateau. The Swedens Cove Trail and the Fern Trail both head out from the camping area and cross TN 156 to reach the South and West Rim Trails. Here, mountain bikers and hikers both cruise the path that circles the steep edge of Swedens Cove. You can gain good views into the lowlands to the southeast toward the Tennessee River and Guntersville Lake. The West Rim Trail heads 6.5 miles to end on TN 156, where you could park a second car to avoid backtracking. However, this area is worth looking over twice. Grab a trail map at the ranger station, which is a log cabin just a bit north of Lake Road on TN 156.

For those seeking shorter hikes, the trail system near the campground offers plenty of options. The trailhead for the Tom Pack Falls Trail is right at the campground. Recommended for hiking only, Tom Pack Falls Trail makes an approximately 2-mile loop down to the falls and back. Another trail rings the unnamed campground lake. After you are done exploring, throw a line from your campsite and see what bites. It may be catfish, bream, or bass.

Other nearby attractions include two caves to explore: one in Carter State Natural Area, the other at Russell Cave National Monument, just a few miles into Alabama. Russell Cave National Monument is a preserved archeological site where Indians lived in pre-Columbian times. History exhibits and ranger-led cave tours enhance the visitor experience.

Franklin State Forest
P.O. Box 68
Winchester, TN 37398

Operated by: Tennessee Division of Forestry

Information: (931) 962-1140

Open: Year-round

Individual sites: 5

Each site has: Picnic table, fire ring

Site assignment: First come, first served; no reservation

Registration: No registration

Facilities: Vault toilet (bring water)

Parking: At campsites only

Fee: None

Elevation: 1,800 feet

Restrictions:

Pets—On 6-foot leash only

Fires—In fire rings only

Alcoholic beverages—Not allowed

Vehicles—Maximum two vehicles per site

Other—14-day stay limit

To get there: Take I-24 Exit 152 south on US Highway 72 to South Pittsburgh. Take TN 156 west then north for 16.7 miles to Lake Road on the left. Take this acute left turn and follow Lake Road 0.7 mile to the main camping area.

FROZEN HEAD STATE PARK

Oak Ridge

F rozen Head is a little-known jewel of a state park tucked away in the Cumberland Mountains, a mountain range west of the Smokies. Steep, forested peaks and deep valleys pocked with rock formations characterize this area, settled in the early 1800s by farmers. But the land, so rich in coal and timber resources, was sold to the state for the establishment of the now infamous Brushy Mountain State Prison, and the resources were extracted using prison labor. The logging era ended in the 1920s and Frozen Head was declared a forest reserve. The Civilian Conservation Corps came in and established many of the trails that are in use today. A plaque at the main trailhead memorializes those who lost their lives developing the area. This is an ideal park for active people who like a small campground but want plenty of activities within walking distance.

Frozen Head's campground is known as the Big Cove Camping Area. A figure-eight loop contains 20 sites that border Big Cove Branch and Flat Fork Creek. Big Cove backs up against Bird Mountain and has a minor slope. The sites have been leveled and are set up amid large boulders that came to rest untold eons ago from atop Bird Mountain. The gray boulders strewn about give it a distinctive Cumberland Mountains feel. Second-growth hardwoods provide ample shade, and the dogwood and hemlock understory allow privacy for campers.

CAMPGROUND RATINGS

Beauty:	★★★★★
Site privacy:	★★★
Site spaciousness:	★★★★
Quiet:	★★★★★
Security:	★★★★★
Cleanliness/upkeep:	★★★★★

Stay at Frozen Head and explore the waterfalls, rock shelters, and mountaintop caprocks of the rugged Cumberland Mountains.

EASTERN

A covered shed contains split firewood for campers to use. The new bathhouse sits close to all in the middle of the campground. Hot showers and flush toilets for each gender are kept in great condition. Two spigots provide drinking water for the small campground. Some sites are fairly close together, but all provide abundant room to spread out your gear. Two group sites are available for $17 per night. Ten sites allow tent and trailer camping; the other nine sites are for tents

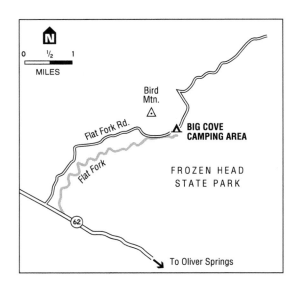

only. An overflow and off-season camping area is situated along Flat Fork Creek up from the regular campground. It has only a camping spot and fire ring.

The park gates are closed from sunset to 8 a.m. Late-arriving campers must open and close the gate as they enter. It's best to get situated for the evening and stay within the park's confines. Actually, if you plan wisely, you won't even have to get back in your car until you leave for good; there's plenty to do here. But if you forgot something, you can purchase supplies back in Oliver Springs, east on TN 62.

The trails of Frozen Head will take you to some fascinating places. The 3,324-foot Frozen Head Fire Tower is the apex of the trail system. You can see the surrounding highlands of the Cumberland Plateau and the Great Smoky Mountains in the distance. Other features include the Chimney Rock, a natural observation point that looks west as far as the eye can see. Or take the Panther Branch Trail 0.6 mile up to DeBord Falls. A mile farther is Emory Gap Falls. The Lookout Tower and Bird Mountain trails leave directly from the campground.

Two miles farther on the Bird Mountain Trail is one of Frozen Head's defining rock formations, Castle Rock. This rock formation extends over 100 feet high and 300 feet wide; with a little imagination you can see the center edifice of the castle with turrets on both ends. These rock formations are the remnants of the erosion-resistant sandstone that covers the Cumberland Plateau. The softer rock and soil below this caprock eroded, leaving rock formations that jut straight out of the land. Bicyclers can stay on the Lookout Tower Trail and pedal all the way to the fire tower. Hikers can take this trail or many others to get their views from the tower.

If you don't feel like hiking or relaxing in the campground, there are many other activities. Play volleyball on one of the sand courts. Throw horseshoes at one of the three pits. Shoot some basketball at the outdoor court. Check out the equipment you need free of charge at the park office. During the summer, the 240-seat amphitheater hosts interpretive talks, slide shows, movies, and music.

I planned my trip to coincide with spring's wildflower display. Frozen Head has one of the richest wildflower areas in the Southeast. Even though I could see purple, yellow, and white symbols of the season from my campground, I did tramp many streamside trails and was glad this piece of the Cumberlands was preserved for all to enjoy.

To get there, from Oak Ridge follow TN 62 west 4 miles to Oliver Springs. Drive 13 miles beyond Oliver Springs and turn right onto Flat Fork Road. A sign for Morgan County Regional Correctional Facility and Frozen Head State Park alert you to the right turn. Follow Flat Fork Road 4 miles to the entrance of Frozen Head State Park. The Visitor Center is on your right.

KEY INFORMATION

Frozen Head State Park
964 Flat Fork Road
Wartburg, TN 37887

Operated by: Tennessee State Parks

Information: (423) 346-3318; www.tnstateparks.com

Open: Mid-March–mid-November

Individual sites: 20

Each site has: Picnic table, fire grate/grill, lantern post, firewood

Site assignment: By reservation at least 2 weeks in advance or first come, first served

Registration: At Visitor Center; reserve by phone, (423) 346-3318

Facilities: Water, flush toilets, hot showers

Parking: At campsites only

Fee: $10 per night for 2 people; 50 cents each additional person over age 7

Elevation: 1,500 feet

Restrictions:

Pets—On leash only

Fires—In fire grates only

Alcoholic beverages—Not allowed

Vehicles—16-foot trailer limit due to narrow bridge crossing

Other—14-day stay limit

GEE CREEK CAMPGROUND

Etowah

CAMPGROUND RATINGS

Beauty:	★★★★★
Site privacy:	★★★★
Site spaciousness:	★★★★★
Quiet:	★★★
Security:	★★★★★
Cleanliness/upkeep:	★★★★★

It will take the Hiwassee River and Gee Creek Wilderness to tear you away from the tall pines of Gee Creek Campground.

Gee Creek Campground lies in a large, wooded flat at the base of Starr Mountain, adjacent to the cold, clear waters of the Hiwassee River. Hundreds of tall pines reach for the sky, providing an ideal amount of shade, yet allowing a cool breeze to drift through the campground. The sites are widely spaced along two loops that meander amid the pines. The clean campsites are placed well apart from each other for a maximum amount of spaciousness. Even without a lot of ground-cover, the sheer number of trees and the distance between sites allow for adequate privacy. You never have to walk too far for water, as spigots are spread out along both loops. The campground is well maintained by state employees. A Tennessee State Park ranger lives across from the campground for added security and emergency assistance. The park office is south on US 411 across the Hiwassee River.

Gee Creek is open all year, yet receives heavy use only on summer weekends. The bathhouse is located near the center of the campground and is open from mid-March to the end of November. In winter, portable toilets are used and showers are unavailable, though drinking water is still provided.

Our visit was during spring. Yellow pollen from the numerous pines dusted my Jeep and all our gear. Dogwoods bloomed above the needle-carpeted forest floor.

EASTERN

Warm air and cool air played tug-of-war for dominance. Squirrels scampered about the campground. Birds flew purposefully from tree to tree. We could sense the rebirth of the mountains around us; it seemed leaves were greening and growing before our very eyes.

The Gee Creek Wilderness is merely a short distance away and certainly worth a visit. Drive back to US 411 and turn right. Then turn right at the sign for Gee Creek after half a mile. Follow the paved road over the

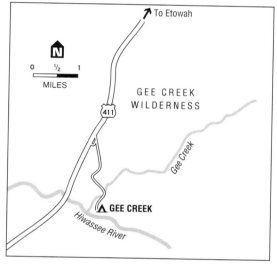

railroad tracks, then turn right. Drive two miles until the road turns to gravel. The Gee Creek Watchable Wildlife Trail is on your left. Just a short distance beyond that is the Gee Creek Trail itself. Trace the old fisherman's trail up the gorge. Small waterfalls provide plentiful photographic opportunities. The trail crosses the creek several times below old-growth hemlocks and dead-ends after 1.9 miles. On the return trip, look for the little things you missed on the way up. Skilled rock climbers can climb some of the creekside bluffs.

The Gee Creek Watchable Wildlife Trail is a 0.7-mile trail designed to increase the hiker's knowledge of nature's signs. The U.S. Forest Service has placed nest boxes, interpretive information, wildlife plantings, and a track pit to see which animals have passed this way. This is an excellent trail to get children interested in nature. Also starting at the Gee Creek trailhead is the Starr Mountain Trail (#190). It leads 4.8 miles up to the ridgeline of Starr Mountain and offers expansive views of the surrounding area.

After all this hiking, maybe you need to cool down. The Hiwassee River awaits and can be enjoyed in a number of ways. It drains over 750,000 acres of forested mountain land, resulting in clear and pure water. Informal trails lead to and along the river from the campground. Make sure young children are supervised. When the turbines upstream are generating, the water will be swift. Most water lovers enjoy the river by raft, canoe, funyak, or tube. No matter your watercraft, it's generally a 5.5-mile float through the splendid Cherokee National Forest. The water, primarily Class I and II on the international scale of difficulty, is very cold. The river is in the last stages of being designated a National Wild and Scenic River. Outfitters will supply anything you need, including a shuttle up the river if you have your own equipment. I recommend Hiwassee Outfitters. They are a reputable family operation. Call (800) 338-8133 for information.

The Hiwassee is also a Mecca for trout fishermen. Anglers head to the river on foggy mornings to dance their flies before unsuspecting trout. If you want to try your luck and are ill-prepared, there are stores and outfitters who will get you on or in the water. The old train depot town of Etowah is 6 miles north on US 411 if you need supplies.

To get there, from Etowah drive south on US 411 for 6 miles. Turn left onto a signed, paved road for Gee Creek Campground and the Cherokee National Forest. Pass through an open field with houses. At one mile turn right into the Gee Creek Campground.

KEY INFORMATION

Gee Creek Campground
Hiwassee State Scenic River,
Box 5
Delano, TN 37325

Operated by: Tennessee State Parks

Information: (423) 263-0050; www.tnstateparks.com

Open: Year-round

Individual sites: 43

Each site has: Picnic table, grill, fire pit, lantern post

Site assignment: First come, first served; no reservations

Registration: With park staffperson on site

Facilities: Drinking water, flush toilets, warm showers, soft drink machines

Parking: At campsites only

Fee: $11 per night for 2 people; 50 cents each additional person

Elevation: 728 feet

Restrictions:

Pets—On leash only

Fires—In fire rings only

Alcoholic beverages—Not allowed

Vehicles—None

Other—14-day stay limit

HOLLY FLATS CAMPGROUND

Tellico Plains

If you place a high priority on barefoot tent camping, skip Holly Flats. True to its name, holly trees dot the cozy Holly Flats Campground, shedding their prickly leaves to decay on the woodland floor. But if you don't mind wearing shoes while you camp, you'll love this place. It offers a variety of sites in a remote atmosphere with plenty to do nearby. The Bald River Gorge Wilderness is just across the gravel road, and Waucheesi Mountain and Warriors Passage National Recreation Trail are close as well.

Holly Flats has that old-time campground ambience: the smell of woodsmoke and hamburgers cooking; sun filtering through the trees; cool mornings and lazy afternoons. This timeworn feel stems from the simple fact that the campground is old. The sites haven't been regraded in a long time, the picnic tables have their share of initials carved in them, and the fire rings are hand-placed, circular piles of rocks. But that's not all bad. The campground is like an old pair of favorite shoes; it may be worn and have a few scuff marks, but it sure is comfortable.

Cross the bridge over Bald River and the campground begins. Two sites are located in the grassy area by the bridge for sun lovers. Farther up, the campground splits into two roads that end in small loops. The first road splits off to the right away from Bald River. It has eight thickly wooded sites

CAMPGROUND RATINGS

Beauty:	★★★★
Site privacy:	★★★★
Site spaciousness:	★★★★★
Quiet:	★★★★★
Security:	★★★
Cleanliness/upkeep:	★★★★

Shoes are a must in this old-time campground next door to the Bald River Wilderness.

EASTERN

spread along a small ridge. These sites offer the most solitude and silence. The farthest site back is atop a small hill away from the road.

The second road runs next to Bald River. All six sites are located directly riverside in a narrow flat. More open, these campsites lay beneath large trees and covered with a holly and rhododendron understory. The melody of the river making its descent permeates the flat. A comfort station with vault toilets for each sex is on the side of the road opposite Bald

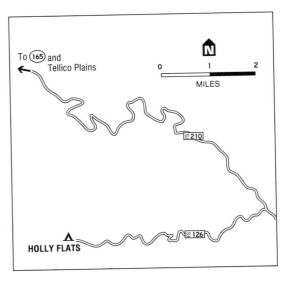

To (165) and Tellico Plains

0   1   2
MILES

FS 210

FS 126

HOLLY FLATS

River. Get your water from an old-fashioned hand pump where the two roads split apart. Holly Flats is a designated pack-it-in, pack-it-out campground. It has no trash receptacles. Pack out all your trash and any trash that thoughtless campers leave behind.

Several hiking trails start near Holly Flats. The Bald River Trail (#88) starts 0.4 mile west down the Bald River on Forest Service Road 126. It strikes through the heart of the 3,700-acre Bald River Gorge Wilderness. The trail leads 4.8 miles through the steep-sided gorge to Bald River Falls. It makes an excellent day hike. For those interested in angling, Bald River is a noted trout stream. The Kirkland Creek Trail (#85) starts 0.4 mile east of the campground on FS 126. A variety of forest types are represented along its route. The trail runs up a valley for three miles, then follows an old logging road to Sandy Gap and the North Carolina state line at 4.6 miles.

Less than one mile east of Holly Flats on FS 126 is the Brookshire Creek Trail (#180). It starts in an old field, crosses Bald River, and climbs six miles to the state line. Brookshire Creek has trout as well. Up the trail are some very remote old homesites where, in times past, subsistence mountain farmers battled the hills and the elements to carve out a living. A clearing lies at the end of the trail and makes a cool summertime picnic spot.

To get a sweat-free overlay of the land, drive to the top of 3,692-foot Waucheesi Mountain. Rangers used to watch for fires from an old tower there. Although it has since been torn down, views are still available from ground level. From Holly Flats drive west on FS 126 to FS 126C. Turn left and climb the mountain; FS 126C ends at the top. You can peer down into the Bald River Gorge and the Tellico River basin. The Warriors Passage National Recreation Trail (#164) starts partway up FS 126C on your right. The trail traces an old route used by the Cherokee on their travels between settlements and, later, by white traders and soldiers who eventually drove the Cherokee out. The historic trail leads one way for five miles to FS 76.

Holly Flats is a relaxing campground bordering one of Tennessee's finest wilderness areas. Give this slice of the Cherokee National Forest a try.

KEY INFORMATION

Holly Flats Campground
250 Ranger Station Road
Tellico Plains, TN 37385

Operated by: U.S. Forest Service

Information: (423) 253-2520; www.southernregion.fs.fed. us/cherokee

Open: Year-round; access road subject to winter closure

Individual sites: 17

Each site has: Tent pad, picnic table, fire ring

Site assignment: First come, first served; no reservations

Registration: Self-registration on site

Facilities: Hand-pumped water, vault toilet

Parking: At campsites only

Fee: $6 per night

Elevation: 2,150 feet

Restrictions:

Pets—On leash only

Fires—In fire rings only

Alcoholic beverages—At campsites only

Vehicles—Parking at sites only

Other—Pack it in; pack it out

To get there, from Tellico Plains drive east on TN 165 for 5.3 miles. Turn right on FS 210. Follow it for 13.9 miles to FS 126. Turn right on gravel FS 126 and follow it for 6 miles. Holly Flats Campground will be across a bridge on your left.

LIMESTONE COVE

Erwin

A tent-camping experience at Limestone Cove is like a trip back in time. This old campground has been here for several decades, an antique camping area if you will. It lies at the base of the Unaka Mountains, a high range dividing North Carolina and Tennessee. Generations of East Tennesseans and western North Carolinians have pitched their tents and relaxed by the curling smoke of a campfire drifting up through the beautiful forest. These locals also know that Limestone Cove makes a great base from which to explore the streams, woodlands and ridgetops of the Unakas. Today, you will find a broken-in yet appealing campground that is worth a night or two of your time.

Limestone Cove is only a stone's throw from TN 107. This two-lane highway sees more traffic than it did during the campground's early days, so you will hear some traffic during your visit. Leave TN 107 and enter the campground. A paved road, covered in part by moss, reveals the extensive shade and lesser use of Limestone Cove. The appeal of the mountain forest is immediately evident. White pines, hemlocks, and hardwoods tower overhead. A thick understory of rhododendron and smaller trees screens the campsites from one another. That, along with ample distance between sites, make for superlative campsite privacy. This separation also makes for

CAMPGROUND RATINGS

Beauty: ★★★★
Site privacy: ★★★★★
Site spaciousness: ★★★★
Quiet: ★★★
Security: ★★
Cleanliness/upkeep: ★★★

Limestone Cove lies at the base of the Unaka Mountain Wilderness.

EASTERN

large campsites. Pass four tent areas, and then come to a vault toilet on the right. Continue on the two-way road, passing more large sites. The rocky forest floor makes the area around the sites a little uneven, but most sites have a level, gravel tent pad. For convenience's sake, each campsite has a litter barrel. Senior citizen national forest volunteers help keep Limestone Cove clean, so help make their job easier by properly disposing of your litter.

As the road descends the valley, more rustic campsites spur from the road until it ends at an auto turnaround. A second vault toilet lies at the lower end of Limestone Cove. Limestone can fill on nice summer weekends but sites are almost always available (excepting holiday weekends and ideal-weather Saturdays during the summer). Consider coming here during the shoulder seasons. Two water spigots are along the campground road, but these have been known to malfunction. Bring your own water just in case.

The Unaka Mountains have been here eons longer than Limestone Cove Campground. However, when the forest service took over the area, they developed some recreation opportunities in the Unakas. Just across TN 107 from the campground is the Limestone Cove Picnic Area. North Indian Creek flows through here. This brook provides quality fishing for rainbow and brown trout. A streamside trail leads to a fishing pier. Trout Unlimited and the forest service have partnered to improve the trout habitat in the Indian Creek.

The Limestone Cove Trail is just up the gravel road from the campground fee station. Pass around the road gate and ascend. The trail veers right from the gated road, and enters the 4,500-acre Unaka Mountain Wilderness. Pass an old homesite. This area is good habitat for bear—one actually skirted the campground while I was there. The trail leads away from Rocky Branch and switchbacks up the mountainside to end after 3.2 miles at Forest Road 230 on Stamping Ground Mountain. FR 230, which is part of the Unaka Mountain Auto Tour, can be reached easier by car. This 30-mile trip takes you past the best auto-accessible sights of the area. Leave the campground and turn right, driving on TN 107 for four miles to Red Fork Road. Turn right here and ascend toward the crest of the Unakas. Pass Clear Fork Creek, a native brook trout stream that the forest service has enhanced as well. Head into the high country and a spruce forest. Stop at the mile-high Unaka Overlook and see out many miles beyond. Drop to Beauty Spot, which lives up to its name. This grassy bald, or field, on top of the mountain offers far-ranging views and beckons visitors to explore the fields and nearby Appalachian Trail on their own. The AT makes for a good hike in either direction. The auto tour reaches TN 395 at Indian Grave Gap and turns right, passing Rock Creek Recreation Area, which has a large natural swimming pool and other amenities. Once in Erwin, turn right on TN 107, passing the Erwin National Fish Hatchery on your left. Check out the trout here. Stay with TN 107 and return to Limestone Cove. After the auto tour, you will realize there is more to see than you thought.

To get there: From exit 23 on US 23 south of Johnson City, take TN 173 south for 1 mile to TN 107. Take TN 107 east for 4 miles to the campground, which will be on your right.

KEY INFORMATION

Limestone Cove
4400 Unicoi Drive
Unicoi, TN 37692

Operated by: U.S. Forest Service

Information: (423) 638-4109; www.southernregion.fs.fed.us/cherokee

Open: May–mid-October

Individual sites: 18

Each site has: Picnic table, fire ring, lantern post

Site assignment: First come, first served; no reservation

Registration: Self-registration on site

Facilities: Vault toilets (bring your own water)

Parking: At campsites only

Fee: $6 per night

Elevation: 2,200 feet

Restrictions:

Pets—On 6-foot leash only

Fires—In fire rings only

Alcoholic beverages—Not allowed

Vehicles—Maximum 2 vehicles per site

Other—14-day stay limit

LITTLE OAK CAMPGROUND

Bristol

Lakeside camping is a breeze at Little Oak. It is sizable and well laid out, lying atop the remnants of Little Oak Mountain after the Holston River Valley was flooded to create South Holston Lake. Though large, Little Oak is widely dispersed on four loops that jut into the lake. This arrangement allows for many spacious lakeside sites, and each loop feels like its own little campground. Short paths slope from each lakeside site to the water's edge. There are so many attractive sites from which to choose. This campground was designed for a pleasant camping experience, not just a way station for the urban masses to cram into. We drove each loop so many times, seeing one ideal site and then seeing an even better one; we were sure another camper was going to turn in our license plate to a ranger.

Just beyond the pay station is the Hemlock Loop. It contains 14 sites nestled beneath a thick stand of hemlock trees. Most of the sites are on the outside of the loop, well away from one another with plenty of cover between sites. An old-fashioned vault toilet and a modern comfort station with flush toilets and showers are at the head of the loop. Camp at Hemlock Loop if you like very shady sites.

Lone Pine Loop is for those who prefer sunny sites. Two small fields lie adjacent to the loop and allow more light into the camping areas. Three comfort stations are

CAMPGROUND RATINGS

Beauty:	★★★★
Site privacy:	★★★★
Site spaciousness:	★★★★
Quiet:	★★★
Security:	★★★★★
Cleanliness/upkeep:	★★★★

Picking the best campsite will be your biggest problem at Little Oak. Both aquatic and earthly endeavors await your arrival.

EASTERN

located by the 16 sites. Only the north end of the loop has lakeside sites.

Big Oak Loop has 16 sites and is located on a spit of hardwoods and evergreens that juts north into the lake. Nearly all the sites are lakeside. A modern comfort station is located halfway along the loop, and water faucets are nearby. The view from Big Oak Loop into South Holston Lake is my personal favorite.

Poplar Loop is the largest with 23 sites, but the sites are split into two loops of

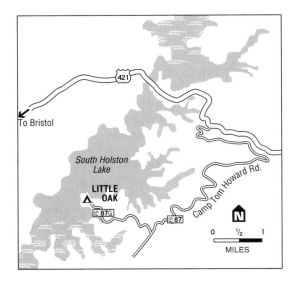

their own, facing west and south into the lake. A modern comfort station can be found at each loop. Most of these sites are lakeside.

We finally settled on Big Oak Loop. After setting up camp, we watched the sun turn into a red ball of fire over South Holston Lake. Gentle waves lapped at our feet as we sat along the shoreline. We took a vigorous hike in the cool of the next morning on the Little Oak Trail that loops the outer peninsula of the campground. This campground is virtually surrounded by the lake, giving it a very aquatic ambience. For a different perspective, take the Little Oak Mountain Trail. It leaves the campground near the pay station and circles back after a jaunt into the woods. For yet another perspective on Little Oak, get out on the lake itself. A boat ramp is conveniently situated between the Hemlock and Poplar loops. Swim, fish, or take a pleasure ride up the lake into the state of Virginia.

In East Tennessee, the high country is never far away. Little Oak is near the Flint Mill Scenic Area, which has a broad representation of Southern Appalachian flora and fauna and elevations exceeding 4,000 feet. Turn right out of the campground onto Forest Service Road 87 and drive a short 1.4 miles. The Josiah Trail (Forest Trail #50) starts on your left and ascends for 2.2 miles to a saddle on Holston Mountain and Forest Trail #44. To your left at 4.3 miles is the Appalachian Trail and the Double Springs Gap backcountry shelter. To your right after 3.4 miles is the Holston Mountain Fire Tower and views aplenty. Flint Mill Trail (FT #49) climbs a steep mile to Flint Rock and some fantastic views of South Holston Lake. The trail is 2.2 miles on the left past the Josiah Trail.

A public pay telephone is located at the pay station. Fishing equipment and all supplies are available back in Bristol.

To get there, from Bristol take US 421 east for 14 miles. Turn right on Camp Tom Howard Road (FS 87) at signed intersection for Little Oak Campground. Follow FS 87 for 6.5 miles. Turn right on FS 87G. Follow it for 1.5 miles and dead-end into Little Oak Recreation Area.

KEY INFORMATION

Little Oak Campground
c/o Watauga Ranger District
USDA Forest Service
P.O. Box 400
Unicoi, TN 37692

Operated by: U.S. Forest Service

Information: (423) 735-1500; www.southernregion.fs.fed.us/cherokee

Open: Late April–November

Individual sites: 72

Each site has: Tent pad, picnic table, fire ring, lantern post

Site assignment: First come, first served; no reservations

Registration: Self-registration on site

Facilities: Water faucets, flush toilets, warm showers

Parking: At campsites only

Fee: $12 per night; $6 when running water is unavailable

Elevation: 1,750 feet

Restrictions:

Pets—On leash only

Fires—In fire rings only

Alcoholic beverages—Not allowed

Vehicles—None

Other—14-day stay limit

NOLICHUCKY GORGE

Erwin

The Nolichucky River cuts a deep gorge through the Appalachian Mountains as it flows from North Carolina into Tennessee. Frothing whitewater tumbles over rocks and boulders beneath towering green ridges. Just a short distance into the Volunteer State, Jones Branch flows into the Nolichucky, creating a riverside flat where Rick Murray, rafter and whitewater man extrordinaire, founded his Nolichucky Gorge Campground. With the exception of a rafting company located next door, the campground overlooking the river is surrounded by national forest land. Having such a neighbor enhances the camping experience here, as rafting the Nolichucky is the primary recreation activity in the gorge. Hiking is also featured here, as the long-distance Appalachian Trail passes a mere 50 yards from the campground, and I am told the fishing can be very good. For those who want a more luxurious tent experience, Rick has installed platform tents—cabin-style tents elevated on wooden platforms and equipped with air mattresses to make your camping even more convenient.

Lets start with the campground. Cross Jones Branch on a small bridge and enter the camping area. Along both sides of the creek are shaded campsites equipped with a platform tent. To the right is the river. A set of nine campsites stretches along the water and offers ideal access and even bet-

CAMPGROUND RATINGS

Beauty:	★★★★
Site privacy:	★★★
Site spaciousness:	★★★★
Quiet:	★★★★
Security:	★★★★
Cleanliness/upkeep:	★★★★★

Raft, hike, fish, and camp in the deep gorge of the Nolichucky River.

EASTERN

ter views of the mountains beyond. Some sites are shaded; others are more in the open. A grassy lawn provides the understory. To your left is a gravel loop road. Here you'll find the campground office, nine RV sites, and four tent sites that are mostly in the open. Backed against the hillside are five shaded tent sites. Also back here are nine more platform tents deep in the shade of pine and tulip trees. Shade lovers will snap up 12 additional tent sites, set deep in more pines, though an open

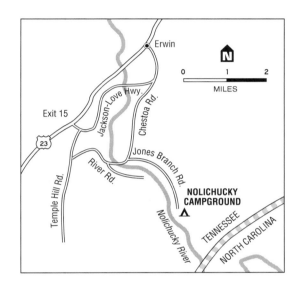

understory cuts down on campsite privacy. Campsite spaciousness is above average on most sites. The bathhouse is located near the campground office. Nolichucky Gorge encourages reservations. When the water is high the campground can fill up, because the Nolichucky Gorge is all about whitewater.

The primary rafting run starts in North Carolina, nine miles upstream. This run offers Class III and IV whitewater and gorge-ous scenery. The "Noli," as it is known among whitewater aficionados, is born on the slopes of Mount Mitchell, highest point in the East, and slices through the Unaka Mountains. The Unakas are mostly forested with serrated outcrops of stone jutting above the trees. Being in national forest land gives the river run a wild and natural aura. Many folks bring their own kayaks and whitewater canoes. Increasing in popularity these days are "funyaks," sort of an inflatable kayak. If you don't have your own boat, walk across Jones Branch to USA Raft. This rafting company uses self-bailing rafts that drain out the water as it splashes overboard. You can also tube downstream from the campground in milder water that is primarily Class II in difficulty.

You don't have to have a boat to enjoy the water. Take a trail from the campground heading upstream along the river to the campground swim beach, where you can intentionally take a dip instead of accidentally falling overboard from a raft. You can also fish the Nolichucky. Trout ply the refreshing waters, as do smallmouth bass, catfish, and muskellunge. Most land-based recreation focuses on the Appalachian Trail. Southbound hikers can wind along the steep cliffs of the Nolichucky Gorge for 1.3 miles to reach the bridge crossing the river over which you drove to the campground. It's a steep climb if you keep going, but you will be rewarded with fine views of the Nolichucky Gorge. Northbound hikers will ascend away from the river to eventually reach Curley Maple Gap trail shelter after three miles, and Indian Grave Gap four miles beyond that. Unless you strap a pack on your back, you'll have a hard time making it to Maine before it is time to turn around. So head back to the Nolichucky Gorge, a fine place to be, whether you are hiking, fishing, or rafting.

To get there: From exit 15 on US 23 near Erwin, head east on Jackson-Love Highway just a short distance to Temple Hill Road. Turn right on Temple Hill Road and follow it for 0.5 mile to River Road. Turn left on River Road and follow it 0.5 mile to Chestoa Pike. Turn left on Chestoa Pike and cross the Nolichucky River to immediately reach Jones Branch Road. Turn right on Jones Branch Road and follow it for 1.3 miles to dead-end at the campground, just beyond the rafting center.

KEY INFORMATION

Nolichucky Gorge
1 Jones Branch Road
Erwin, TN 37650

Operated by: Ricky Murray

Information: (423) 743-8876

Open: Year-round

Individual sites: 31 tent sites, 15 platform tent sites, 8 RV sites

Each site has: Picnic table, fire ring

Site assignment: First come, first served and by reservation

Registration: At campground office

Facilities: Hot showers, flush toilets, water spigots

Parking: At campsites only

Fee: $8 per person per night; $10 per person per night for platform tents

Elevation: 1,750 feet

Restrictions:

Pets—On 6-foot leash only

Fires—In fire rings only

Alcoholic beverages—At campsites only

Vehicles—None

Other—None

NORRIS DAM STATE PARK

Lake City

There is so much to do at Norris Dam State Park and environs that it's hard to know where to begin. What started as a flood control project during the Great Depression has resulted in a park with lake, river, and land recreation administered by the state of Tennessee and the Tennessee Valley Authority (TVA). During the flood control project development, the pioneer history of the Clinch River Valley was evident, thus a special emphasis was placed on preserving the past as changes were made. Today, we have the Lenoir Pioneer Museum, an 18th-century gristmill, a threshing barn, and outside the park boundaries, one of East Tennessee's most rewarding attractions, the Museum of Appalachia.

But there is a drawback. The two park campgrounds are just a slice above run-of-the mill. In fact, one of them, the West Campground, isn't worth visiting to seek a site, at least for us tent campers. However, the East Campground has a primitive area that makes the overnighting experience here better than tolerable. Coming from Norris, you will turn right into the east park entrance just before reaching the dam. (The West End Campground is a few miles farther. It has 50 overly crowded RV sites atop a hill with little shade. Don't bother unless you are sizing up RVs to buy.) Drive on up and turn into the East Campground. It is a little too cramped, too

CAMPGROUND RATINGS

Beauty:	★★★
Site privacy:	★★★
Site spaciousness:	★★★★
Quiet:	★★★★
Security:	★★★★
Cleanliness/upkeep:	★★★★

Pioneer history and natural activities are abundant around the site of the Tennessee Valley Authority's first dam.

EASTERN

open, and under a power-line. Not good. Paved pads, water, and electricity add up to make this RV heaven. But some sites are adequately spaced and a determined tent camper can find decent camping here. A road spurs right, down to thick woods. This is the Primitive Camping Area. Here in the shade are unnumbered, informal sites, with picnic tables and rock fire rings. Most of the sites are level enough to avoid tossing and turning at night. More sites are adjacent to the gravel loop road

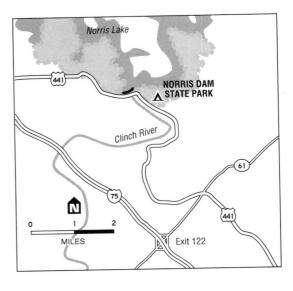

that climbs back toward the main campground. Of interest is one campsite atop the hill by the powerline that is appealing for its solitude. A bathhouse centers the main camping loop. Primitive sites are available year-round, save for holiday weekends.

Now to the good stuff. Norris Lake, the result of Norris Dam, is one of the most attractive lakes in the South. A boating experience of any kind is bound to be a good one, whether it is skiing, fishing or just pleasure cruising. A commercial marina, on the far side of the dam from East Campground, will serve your boating needs. The Clinch River flows from beneath the dam. Many die-hard anglers tout its cold waters to be the finest trout fishery in the state. I have to agree; I have caught my share of trout on many a float-fishing trip down this river. If you are more land-oriented, paths galore will keep you coming back for more. Four distinct trail systems course through the area. The CCC Camp Trail System, developed in the 1930s along with the dam, is near the East Campground. Several interconnected trails make loop possibilities. The High Point Trail extends nearly four miles and is open to mountain bikes.

The Andrews Ridge Trail System is near the West Campground. It winds through a younger forest once farmed by families that were relocated during the damming. The Park Headquarters Trail System has the Fitness Trail with exercise stations. The TVA Trail system includes the River Bluff Trail, which travels along the Clinch River.

History buffs should visit the privately owned Museum of Appalachia. Owner John Rice Irwin truly takes pride in this region and it shows; the 65-acre destination must be seen to be appreciated. Inside the park boundaries is the Lenoir Museum. It gives a pictorial history of the area in pre-dam days. Also nearby here are the threshing barn and old gristmill, which operates during summer. Ranger-led activities, conducted Wednesday through Sunday during summer, include rappelling, trips to Hill Cave, and a lake cruise where you can learn about the history of Norris Dam. One thing you won't hear on a tent-camping trip here is, "I'm bored. There's nothing to do."

To get there: From exit 122 on I-75 near Norris, head west on TN 61 for 1.4 miles to US 441. Turn left on 441 and follow it for 6 miles to the East Campground adjacent to Norris Dam.

KEY INFORMATION

Norris Dam State Park
125 Village Green Circle
Lake City, TN 37769

Operated by: Tennessee State Parks

Information: (865) 426-7461; www.tnstateparks.com

Open: Year-round

Individual sites: East Campground, 10 primitive sites, 25 other; West Campground, 50 other

Each site has: Primitive sites have picnic table, fire ring; others have water and electricity

Site assignment: First come, first served; no reservation

Registration: At park office or ranger will come by and register you

Facilities: Hot showers, flush toilets, water spigots, laundry, pay phone

Parking: At campsites only

Fee: $10.50 per night primitive sites, $14 per night water and electric sites for tents

Elevation: 1,100 feet

Restrictions:

Pets—On 6-foot leash only

Fires—In fire rings only

Alcoholic beverages—Not allowed

Vehicles—Trail, bikes, minibikes and ATVs prohibited

Other—14-day stay limit

OBED WILD AND SCENIC RIVER

Wartburg

The Obed National Wild and Scenic River, administered by the National Park Service, has come of age. What once was a protected recreation area in name only has now evolved into a multiple outdoor activity destination supported by the community. It all began with die-hard kayakers and canoers plying the whitewater of the Obed-Emory River watershed. Next a few paddle access points were established. Then a 14-mile segment of the Cumberland Trail was completed, running through the heart of the Obed River gorge. The addition of Rock Creek Campground at the Nemo Bridge boat access has made this scenic swath of the Cumberland Plateau a prime destination for tent campers.

When I started coming here nearly two decades ago, the Nemo Bridge area was a local party spot. Boy, have things changed. The old boat access is now a nice picnic area and trailhead. The old Nemo Bridge is used for foot traffic only. Continue across the new bridge and turn right, and descend into the campground. Upon entering the campground, the quality design of Rock Creek Campground is immediately evident. Each site is clearly delineated with landscaping timbers, and raised tent pads filled with coarse sand offers quick drainage and easy staking of your tent. The stone picnic tables are embellished with designs, much as you would see in a garden at home. The fire

CAMPGROUND RATINGS

Beauty:	★★★★★
Site privacy:	★★★
Site spaciousness:	★★★
Quiet:	★★★★
Security:	★★★
Cleanliness/upkeep:	★★★★

Enjoy the wonders of the wild and scenic Obed River from this new campground.

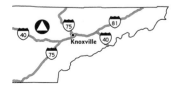

EASTERN

rings and lantern posts are placed to last a long time.

Cross clear Rock Creek and spy the self-service fee station dead ahead. To the left is a single campsite that offers the most privacy. Turn right to enter a tall woodland of sycamore and tulip trees, and pass the Cumberland Trail, which conveniently leaves directly from the camping area. One site lies near the trail. Pass two vault toilets, and then come to two nice campsites that are just a stone's throw from the Obed River. A nature trail heads upriver beyond these two campsites.

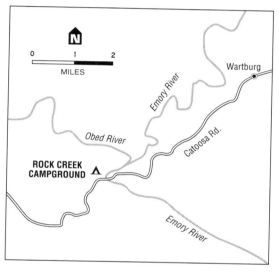

Continue to curve along the river and come to site 5. It is also close to the river and near Rock Creek as well. Pass two more good sites, then come to a set of three walk-in tent campsites. Two wooden bridges span a wet-weather drainage to access the shady sites complemented by some hemlocks and rhododendron. The final site is handicap accessible. Campers should be able to find a site most any weekend if they arrive on Friday. Getting a site is no problem during weekdays and the fall and winter seasons. Summer weekdays are good, too. Plan to scramble for a site on spring weekends when the water is right for paddling.

So what about all this great recreation here? The Obed is really comprised of four drainages that offer paddling of varying difficulties. These watercourses—Daddys Creek, Clear Creek, Emory River and the Obed River—have cut gorges into the Cumberland Plateau, where bluffs overlook rock-choked rivers lying beside thick forests. Upper Daddy's Creek is for experts only, but the last two miles of this river, from the Devils Breakfast Table on, are Class II water, as is the

Emory River from Nemo Bridge to Oak-dale. Just watch for that first rapid, Nemo; it has flipped me a few times. Some sections of Clear Creek are doable by average boaters, but other runs are tough. If you are going to paddle, go with someone who knows the water on your initial trips, and call the visitor center for water levels.

The rivers are good for fishing, too. Muskie, bass, bream, and catfish await in the river's deeper holes, though most of these are accessible by self-propelled boat or foot only. This unit of the national park service also has a good walk for you. Take the Cumberland Trail from the campground up the Emory River, climbing away from the water before reaching its confluence with the Obed. At 2.6 miles you will near Alley Ford. Another two miles will take you to Breakaway Bluff Overlook. The trail travels on to Rock Garden Overlook and views of rapids before picking up an old railroad bed. It ends after 14 miles at the Devils Breakfast Table on Daddys Creek. If this one-way trek is too far, consider driving to the Devils Breakfast Table and starting down Daddys Creek, where two overlooks await in the first mile and the Rain House, a rock shelter, is a mile farther. Pick up a trail map and park map at the visitor center in Wartburg. A shorter option might take the Cumberland Trail up the Emory to a nature trail that leaves right and descends to end up at the campground near the water's edge. No matter which option you choose, grab your tent and head for the Obed.

To get there: From the Obed Visitor Center next to the courthouse in downtown Wartburg, take Maiden Street west two blocks to Catoosa Road. Turn right on Catoosa Road and follow it 6 miles to the campground, which is on the right just past the bridge over the Emory River.

KEY INFORMATION

Obed Wild and Scenic River
P.O. Box 429, 208 N. Maiden St.
Wartburg, TN 37887

Operated by: National Park Service

Information: (423) 346-6294, www.nps.gov/obed

Open: Year-round

Individual sites: 12

Each site has: Picnic table, fire ring, lantern post, tent pad

Site assignment: First come, first served; no reservation

Registration: Self-registration on site

Facilities: Vault toilets (bring your own water)

Parking: At campsites only

Fee: $7 per night

Elevation: 900 feet

Restrictions:

Pets—On 6-foot leash only

Fires—In fire rings only

Alcoholic beverages—At campsites only

Vehicles—Maximum 2 vehicles per site

Other—14-day stay limit

PICKETT STATE PARK

Jamestown

Tennessee State Parks come fully loaded with man-made amenities to make the most of your visit. But Pickett State Park was already fully loaded with natural features long before it became Tennessee's first state park way back in the 1930s. The campground is vintage, too. It is evident that over the years, Pickett's natural beauty, as well as the campground, have passed through caring hands.

The campground is situated atop a wooded hill. It has the standard circular loop configuration with a road bisecting the center of the loop, making almost a figure eight. You'll climb as you enter the loop. Most sites are on the outer edge of the loop, but the road that bisects the loop also has campsites along it. Tall pines and hardwoods shade the camping area. A light understory is prevalent, mixed with more heavily wooded sections, especially outside the main loop.

The campground was built before RVs existed, so, even though 31 of 32 sites have both water and electricity, it is primarily a tenter's campground. Water is nearby for the other nine sites. A modern bathhouse with flush toilets, hot showers, and a coin laundry are in the very center of the campground. Those staying on the campground's perimeter may have to walk a bit to reach the bathhouse.

Hand-laid stone walls complement their natural surroundings. The campground

CAMPGROUND RATINGS

Beauty:	★★★★
Site privacy:	★★★
Site spaciousness:	★★★
Quiet:	★★★★
Security:	★★★★★
Cleanliness/upkeep:	★★★★

Tennessee's first state park is 11,750 acres of scenic botanical and geologic wonders.

EASTERN

blends in well, too. Even the park water tank is overlaid with stone. The campsites are a bit smaller than normal, but they offer more than adequate space. It's quiet and secure here in the outer reaches of Fentress County, adjacent to the Kentucky state line. A park ranger lives on site at the state park and the Visitor Center is nearby should you need assistance.

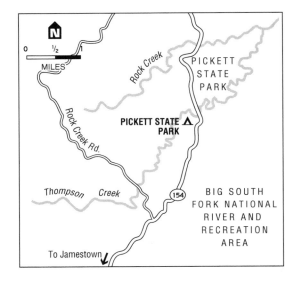

You may need help figuring out just what to do. Man-made pursuits include tennis, badminton, horseshoes, and volleyball. Any equipment you may need is available free of charge at the park office. Though not a wooded health club, there's still plenty of man-made fun to enhance the natural recreation available.

A swimming beach is open during the summer months at Arch Lake. This 15-acre, S-shaped lake offers trout fishing and canoe and rowboat rentals. A park naturalist is on duty during the summer. Headquarters are at the nature center, which is in the middle of the campground. Campfire programs and movies are also part of Pickett activities.

Finally, there are the landforms, without which no man-made state park could've been created. Much of the state forest escaped the logger's ax. Today, over 58 miles of trails trace beneath the trees, reaching natural bridges, caves, waterfalls, and rock bluffs.

Several short trails serve to loosen your legs. The Indian Rockhouse Trail travels 0.2 mile to a huge rock overhang with a water feature in its center. The 2.5-mile Lake Trail Loop crosses Arch Lake on a swinging bridge, then passes a natural bridge before looping back to the picnic area; it is one mile down to

Double Falls from Thompson Overlook. The Hazard Cave Loop extends for 2.5 miles and goes by a sand-floored cave, then by the Natural Bridge, over 80 feet long and 20 feet high.

The two primary park trails are Rock Creek and Hidden Passage. The Rock Creek Trail parallels its namesake, passing small waterfalls in a classic, deeply wooded mountain stream. The trail is five miles one way and connects to the Sheltowee Trace Trail. The Sheltowee Trace Trail extends 250 miles into Kentucky. Sheltowee is Indian for "Big Turtle," which is what the local Indians called Daniel Boone way back when he was adopted into the Shawnee Tribe.

The master trail of Pickett is the 10-mile Hidden Passage Trail. The first feature you'll see is a modest arch, then comes the Hidden Passage, a small passageway created by a large rock overhang amid jumbled rocks. Next is Crystal Falls. On down you'll see overlooks and numerous rock houses, some with chestnut benches built by the Civilian Conservation Corps during the Depression. Take the Hidden Passage challenge. It will be a day to remember.

A rough trail map is available at the Visitor Center. They'll be glad to help you find a trail to suit your desires. This is one place where you can stay busy for days with all types of activities. Just make sure to get all your food and supplies back in Jamestown. You'll need the calories.

KEY INFORMATION

Pickett State Park
Polk Creek Route, Box 174
Jamestown, TN 38556

Operated by: Tennessee State Parks

Information: (931) 879-5821; www.tnstateparks.com

Open: Year-round

Individual sites: 32

Each site has: Tent pad, fire grate, lantern post, picnic table

Site assignment: First come, first served; no reservations

Registration: At Visitor Center

Facilities: Water, flush toilets, showers, laundry, electrical hookups

Parking: At campsites only

Fee: $11 per night for 2 people; 50 cents each additional person

Elevation: 1,500 feet

Restrictions:

Pets—On leash only

Fires—In fire grates only

Alcoholic beverages—Not allowed

Vehicles—None

Other—14-day stay limit

To get there, from Jamestown take US 127 north for 2 miles to TN 154. Turn right on TN 154 and follow it for 10 miles. The park entrance will be on your left.

PRENTICE COOPER STATE FOREST

Chattanooga

Perched atop Suck Creek Mountain, overlooking the Grand Canyon of the Tennessee River, 26,000-acre Prentice Cooper is a surprisingly quiet getaway for nearby Chattanooga residents. It was once a hunting ground of the Cherokee Indians, who lived along the banks of the Tennessee River where Chattanooga now lies. Later, Europeans settled here, logging the land and using it for grazing livestock. The state took over these once-abused lands in the late 1930s and now manages the land for forestry and hunting. Prentice Cooper is also home to the southern terminus of the Cumberland Trail, which is slated to run the length of the Cumberland Plateau all the way to Cumberland Gap National Historic Park in Kentucky.

Davis Pond campsite is small, with only a couple of developed sites, though at least two other groups could easily squeeze into the camping area. Set up your camp beside this man-made pond and break out the boots to enjoy nearly 40 miles of trails offering views from places like Snoopers Rock, set on the rim of the gorge. Mountain bikers can ride numerous forest roads that spur off the primary Tower Road. No matter your mode of exploration, downtown Chattanooga will seem far, far away.

The Davis Pond campsite is the only auto-accessible campsite in the forest. It is situated on a flattened ridge atop Suck Creek Mountain. Posts ring the gravel

CAMPGROUND RATINGS

Beauty:	★★★★
Site privacy:	★★★
Site spaciousness:	★★★★
Quiet:	★★★★★
Security:	★★★★
Cleanliness/upkeep:	★★★

The campground is small, but there's big hiking to be had along the Tennessee River Gorge.

EASTERN

parking area, keeping cars where they belong. On the far side of the posts lies the camping area, an alluring grassy spot with scattered shade trees backed by a rising wooded hill. Davis Pond, around one acre in size, forms one border of the campground. To the left, near to the campground entrance road, is a vault toilet. Beyond the toilet is the first developed campsite with a picnic table and rock fire ring. Overhead are shade-bearing pines. The other developed site is closer to Davis Pond.

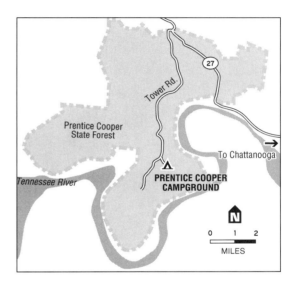

Both these sites require a short walk from your car. The rest of the campground is suitable for a few other tents, so don't despair if the two sites are taken. There is no water here, only a vault toilet, but there is a pump well at the gated entrance to the state forest. Speaking of this gate, it closes at sunset, and the state forest asks you to be at your campsite by sunset and don't expect to leave until sunrise. This is done to cut down on poaching. Also, be apprised of spring and fall managed hunts in the forest. These hunts are posted on the web at www.cumberlandtrail.org. Or just call Tennessee Wildlife Resources Agency. Avoid Prentice Cooper on these weekends. During the week, the state forest will be your own. So get out there and hit the trail.

The nearest hiking, the Pot Point Trail, is back a bit on Tower Road. This trail makes a half-mile run to Snoopers Rock, picks up the Cumberland Trail, then cruises south along the Grand Canyon of the Tennessee River, passing Pot Point and a thirty-foot high natural bridge. More overlooks await before the trail turns up McNabb Gulf and crosses Tower Road, where you can complete your loop. The Mullens Cove Loop is shorter at 10 miles; it intersects the Cumberland Trail at Indian Rockhouse and runs the gorge line of the Tennessee River before looping around and up the Mullens Creek Gorge. Other closed jeep roads can make shorter loops for hikers or bikers. No matter what path you take, this mountaintop forest will not fail to please the eye.

To get there: From the junction with Main Street near downtown Chattanooga, take US 27 north for 3 miles to US 127 north. Take US 127 north for 1.6 miles to TN 27 west. Turn left on TN 27 west and follow it for 8 miles to Choctow Trace Road. Turn left on Choctow Trace Road and follow it for 0.2 mile to reach Game Reserve Road. Turn left on Game Reserve Road and enter Prentice Cooper State Forest, where it becomes Tower Road. Keep forward on Tower Road for 7 miles to reach Davis Pond Road. Turn left on Davis Pond Road and follow it 0.6 mile to reach the campground, on your left.

KEY INFORMATION

Prentice Cooper State Forest
P.O. Box 160
Hixson, TN 37343

Operated by: Tennessee Division of Forestry

Information: (423) 634-3091

Open: Year-round

Individual sites: 4

Each site has: Picnic table, fire ring

Site assignment: First come, first served; no reservation

Registration: No registration

Facilities: Vault toilet (bring your own water)

Parking: In campground parking area only

Fee: None

Elevation: 1,750 feet

Restrictions:

Pets—On 6-foot leash only

Fires—In fire rings only

Alcoholic beverages—Not allowed

Vehicles—None

Other—Campers must be at campsite by sunset, as entrance gates close until sunrise

ROUND MOUNTAIN CAMPGROUND

Newport

Round Mountain Campground is off the beaten path in a seemingly forgotten corner of the Bald Mountains in Cherokee National Forest. Maybe it is the tortuously twisting gravel road that keeps visitation minimal up there. We stayed there on a Friday night with good weather in mid-June, and only three of the 16 sites were occupied. The three other groups were tent campers. Those who find Round Mountain will relish the tranquil high-country campground so in tune with the woods that it seems to have been constructed by Mother Nature.

The sites of Round Mountain are intermittently located on a single, thickly forested loop road that is bordered in moss—you are literally in the woods. Tall trees, including high-elevation species such as yellow birch and pin cherry, intermingle with hemlock and white pine to provide a thick overhead canopy, shading all campers and the loop road. Junglesque growth of rhododendron on the forest floor buffers campers from one another. Noisy little streams cascade down the mountainside amid the brush.

The first two campsites are actually located on the approach road to the loop. The next five sites are placed where possible between large trees and dense undergrowth. You must climb some steps to reach the campground's most isolated site. One other walk-up site is available. The

CAMPGROUND RATINGS

Beauty:	★★★★★
Site privacy:	★★★★★
Site spaciousness:	★★★★★
Quiet:	★★★★★
Security:	★★★★
Cleanliness/upkeep:	★★★★★

The must-see mountain meadow of Max Patch and lofty, wooded camping await those willing to tackle the long and winding gravel access road.

EASTERN

additional sites lie along the loop where they blend in well with the scenery, keeping plenty of distance between each other for maximum privacy.

A traditional hand-pump well emits cool mountain water. The pump is located at the beginning of the loop, along with a comfort station with clean vault toilets for each gender. Make your last supply stop in Newport and don't plan on coming off Round Mountain until your stay is over. That winding road to and from civilization

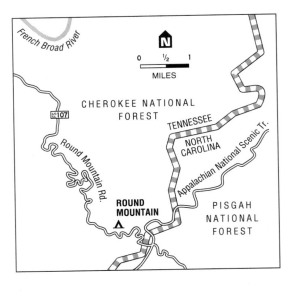

is a bear. Also, be certain to call ahead and verify that the campground is open if you plan to visit in early spring or late fall.

It is just a short distance from the campground to the Walnut Mountain Trail. Walk out to Forest Service Road 107, then go downhill 30 yards to reach the trailhead. It leads one mile to Rattlesnake Gap and another mile to the Appalachian Trail near the Walnut Mountain shelter. Attractive scenery is a safe bet either way you turn on the AT from there.

Our June journey took place on a cool mountain morning. Sunlight penetrated the forest canopy here and there, illuminating a light mist that rose from the woodland floor. The famed Max Patch was waiting. We turned left out of the campground on FS 107, motoring two miles up to Lemon Gap and the North Carolina border. Naturally, the Appalachian Trail threaded through these lovely groves, as it does in so many of the Southern Appalachians' treasure spots. On we drove, veering right at Lemon Gap on FS 1182 and driving 3.5 miles farther, past a trout pond maintained by the Pisgah National Forest. Old-timers in overalls lounged in lawn chairs beside fishing poles with lines in the pond.

Beyond the pond, the forest opened to our left, revealing Max Patch in all its glory. The 230-acre field was once part of a working farm; the field now supports only wildflowers, which bloomed by the thousands, all facing the morning sun. We crested the top of the field at 4,629 feet and were rewarded with a 360° view. To the south stood the Great Smoky Mountains. Mount Sterling, with its metal fire tower, and Mount Cammerer, with its distinctive stone tower, stood out among the countless peaks. The open fields of the Bald Mountains stretched out to the north. It seemed as if we were in the very heart of the Southern Appalachians. We may well have been.

Round Mountain is my favorite campground in this entire guidebook. Between the quiet solitude and classic, high-country atmosphere of each campsite and the magnificence of Max Patch, this area exudes the best of the uplands that extend from the North Woods into Dixie. After all, it is hard to go wrong combining the beauty of the Appalachians and the charm of the South.

KEY INFORMATION

Round Mountain Campground
124 Austin Street, Suite 3
Greeneville, TN 37743

Operated by: U.S. Forest Service

Information: (423) 638-4109; www.southernregion.fs.fed.us/cherokee

Open: Mid-May–mid-December

Individual sites: 16

Each site has: Tent pad, fire grate, lantern post, picnic table, stand-up grill

Site assignment: First come, first served; no reservations

Registration: Self-registration on site

Facilities: Hand-pumped water, vault toilets

Parking: At campsites only

Fee: $7 per night

Elevation: 3,000 feet

Restrictions:

Pets—On 6-foot or shorter leash

Fires—In fire grates only

Alcoholic beverages—At campsites only

Vehicles—22-foot trailer limit

Other—14-day stay limit

To get there, from Newport take US 25/70 for 10 miles to TN 107 at Del Rio. Turn right on TN 107 and follow it for 5.8 miles. Turn left on gravel FS 107 (Round Mountain Road) as it climbs Round Mountain. After 6 miles, Round Mountain Campground will be on your left.

SYLCO CAMPGROUND

Benton

If you place a high priority on quiet solitude and close-at-hand wilderness hiking, Sylco is just the place for you. It is located in an isolated area of the Cherokee National Forest in the extreme southeastern corner of Tennessee. You don't have to worry about RVs or trailers coming to this campground. There are three ways to get in here, and each way is rough and remote, just like the Sylco area. Then out of nowhere, in the middle of nowhere, appears a grassy plot of land interspersed with shade trees and picnic tables. Just make sure you have all your supplies.

Primarily used as a hunting camp in fall, this campground is very lightly used the rest of the year. It is so lightly used that the Forest Service doesn't even charge campers to stay here. And only a few of the 12 sites appear to get enough use to even beat down the grass that grows around the picnic tables.

It's remote—no registration and no campground hosts. Some sites don't even have both a picnic table and grill; some just have a fire ring with the table. There's even one grill with no table. You'll find no tent pads either. Just pitch your tent right on the grass; it may slope a bit. This is the most primitive campground in this guidebook. Not to say this place is ragged and neglected; it's just remote—and clean.

Surrounded by second-growth forest, the campground is in a dry, mid-mountain

CAMPGROUND RATINGS

Beauty:	★★★★
Site privacy:	★★★★
Site spaciousness:	★★★★★
Quiet:	★★★★★
Security:	★★
Cleanliness/upkeep:	★★★★

Sylco, near the Big Frog and Cohutta wildernesses, is the most primitive campground in this guidebook.

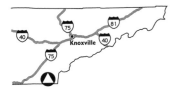

EASTERN

slope area that has been selectively cleared of trees, leaving tall oaks and pines to partially shade the grassy campsites below. There's no understory between the spacious and open sites to shield you from other campers, but there probably won't be any other campers—you'll have wild animals for company and birds will be your noisy neighbors.

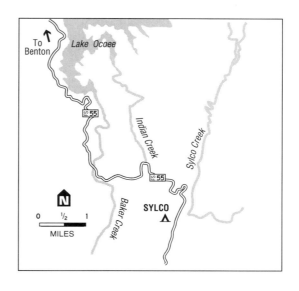

This lightly used campground extends onto both sides of the road. A short loop swings by the four sites on the downslope. Their tables are fairly close together, so the sites could be suitable for a group camp. A larger loop circles around the upper eight sites. All but one of the sites are in the center of the loop. None of the sites have an official parking spur. Pull over to one side of the loop or just park in the grass. Only two of the sites appear to have been used in recent years, and they have parking areas. A vault toilet for each gender stands at the high point of the upper loop.

The campground has no Forest Service–provided water. But nature will provide you with some in case you left yours behind. A narrow path leads 75 yards downslope from the lowest picnic table of the lower loop to a small clear stream. To be on the safe side, treat or boil this water.

Sylco makes a great base camp for the area's wilderness hiking, trout and smallmouth bass fishing, and forest drives. But you'll need a Forest Service map of the Cherokee to make your way around. Big Frog and Cohutta form a 45,000-acre wilderness area (plenty of room for a bear or two). Three miles south of Sylco is Jacks River and the Cohutta Wilderness in Georgia. The Jacks River Trail (Forest Trail #13) follows an old railroad bed, crossing Jacks River many times. Look for rotting crossties and old railroad spikes. Trout and some especially aggressive smallmouth bass dwell here. The eight-mile hike to Jacks River Falls is worth the 20 fords.

If you like the view from up high, take one of the trails that lead to the top of Big Frog Mountain (4,224 feet), centerpiece of the Big Frog Wilderness. Take the Chestnut Mountain Trail (FT #63) and climb the mountain connecting the Wolf Ridge Trail for a 3.7-mile hike to the mountaintop. Another fine route uses Big Creek Trail (FT #68) connecting to Barkleggin Trail, then to Big Frog via Big Frog Trail. Big Creek offers quality trout fishing as well.

Excellent forest drives can be used to loop back to Sylco. No four-wheel-drive vehicles are necessary. Peavine Road (Forest Service Road 221) leads back to US 64 and the famed Ocoee River. Big Frog Road (FS 62) skirts Big Frog and Cohutta wildernesses offering a taste of the wild without leaving your vehicle. Go slow, ignore the bumps, and try to keep your eyes on the road as well as the scenery.

KEY INFORMATION

Sylco Campground
Route 1, Box 348D
Benton, TN 37307

Operated by: U.S. Forest Service

Information: (423) 338-5201; www.southernregion.fs.fed. us/cherokee

Open: Year-round

Individual sites: 12

Each site has: Picnic table, grill

Site assignment: First come, first served; no reservations

Registration: Not necessary

Facilities: Vault toilet

Parking: At campsites

Fee: None

Elevation: 1,200 feet

Restrictions:

Pets—On leash only

Fires—In fire rings only

Alcoholic beverages—Not allowed

Vehicles—parking at sites only

To get there, from Benton drive south on US 411 2 miles to US 64. Take US 64 east for 6 miles to the Ocoee District Ranger Station. Buy a map of the Cherokee National Forest. From the Ranger Station, take US 64 west for 4.9 miles. Turn left on Cookson Creek/Baker's Creek Road for 3.5 miles to national forest boundary; at boundary, Baker's Creek Road becomes FS 55. Continue on FS 55 for 6.5 miles to Sylco.

WESTERN
KENTUCKY

BIRMINGHAM FERRY

Lake City

The north end of Land Between the Lakes is really more than land between Kentucky Lake and Lake Barkley. It is enveloped on three sides by water: Lake Barkely covers the land's east flank as well as curving around and circling its north side. Kentucky Lake forms the western border. This area should be called Land Darn Near Encircled by Lakes. Like the rest of Land Between the Lakes, the north end is rife with recreational opportunities and a few good campgrounds. But the best campground destination for tent campers is Birmingham Ferry. It is moderately sized, rustic, and has many lakeside camp-sites. All sorts of watery recreation oppor-tunities are at hand, with trails for mountain bikers just a pedal away. These trails are open to hikers as well.

Old Ferry Road ends near Kentucky Lake and enters the campground. The first cou-ple of sites in the loop are wide open and away from the lake—a whole 100 feet from the water. A few trees begin to shade some of the later sites, but then the loop turns left toward the water, where seven large, some-what open sites lie directly on the water.

In the middle of the loop, a road contin-ues away from the water. Climb a small ridge on this road and dip again to the lake, this time into Pisgah Bay. Drop down to the water and there are two isolated sites right on the lake. Boaters claim these sites early. Pass the boat ramp and boater parking area

CAMPGROUND RATINGS

Beauty:	★★★★
Site privacy:	★★★
Site spaciousness:	★★★
Quiet:	★★★★
Security:	★★★
Cleanliness/upkeep:	★★★★

Camp here to enjoy the north end of Land Between the Lakes.

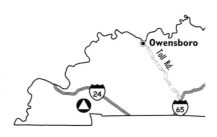

WESTERN

and come to an unlikely loop on an ultra-steep hill. Here, two bluff-side sites offer a great view, but make sure and tie yourself in or you might take a tumble. These sites are not suitable for kids. Swing around and climb higher on the hill to a couple more sites on a more reasonable slope. The sites themselves have been leveled out.

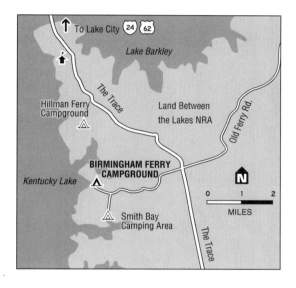

Nearby, just a ridge over to the south, is the Smith Bay Camping Area. You may want to look this over before you make your final campsite decision. Pass Campsite 16, all by itself on the water, then come to the boat launch. Enter the main campground. It is very open, but it usually has a shade tree or two to keep the sun at bay. Pass by a string of seven lakeside sites, then turn away from the water and go uphill to see a few more sites. These sites are better shaded but still have a view of Smith Bay, and like Birmingham Ferry, have convenient vault toilets and a water spigot.

Water recreation is just a walk away from your tent from either campground. Boating, fishing, and swimming are likely choices. The reason I prefer Birmingham Ferry is the added land-based recreation. The North-South Trail crosses Old Ferry Road just a half-mile from the campground. Open to hikers and mountain bikers, you can walk or pedal straight from the campground. Head south toward Hatchery Hollow and the Nature Station Connector Trail, where there are paths aplenty. If you head north, you will come to a side trail reaching Nightriders Spring, then a paved hike/bike trail that makes a loop out of Hillmans Ferry. Farther north are the Canal Loop trails. A series of connector trails make loop routes possible here, ranging from 1.5 miles to 10 or more miles. Wear yourself out, but first get a trail map at the north entrance station to know where you are going. After a tent camping adventure at Birmingham Ferry, you are sure to grab your friends and come back for more.

To get there: From exit 31 on I-24 near Lake City, head south on KY 453 for 11.7 miles, intersecting the Trace along the way to reach Old Ferry Road (FS 114). Turn right on Old Ferry Road and follow it 3.5 miles to dead-end at the campground.

COLUMBUS-BELMONT STATE PARK

Columbus

You won't believe the trees at this park. There are some huge ones—cottonwoods, sugar maples, and oaks—throughout this preserve located on dramatic bluffs of the Mississippi River. If it's summer during your visit, you will enjoy the shade of one of these trees while overlooking the Big Muddy and the state of Missouri beyond. Mother Nature had a direct hand in creating this state park. In April of 1927, the Mississippi River flooded the nearby town of Columbus. The Red Cross subsequently sent a fellow named Rust to help; he got the town relocated to higher, less flood-prone ground, where it stands today. While relocating the town, Rust became interested in the remains of the Confederate fortifications here and thought these fortifications worth preserving. After Rust's efforts, the Civilian Conservation Corps came in and helped develop the park that makes for Western Kentucky's best camping destination.

The park campground is situated on a high bluff several hundred feet above the mighty Mississippi. The campsite numbering system is odd. You have 1 on one side and 38 directly across the road. Of course, numbers don't matter; it's the site that counts. Head up a hill beneath large shade trees such as sweetgum and oak mixed with lush grassy areas. The first few sites on the right are "pull-beside" sites next to the park road and are the least desirable.

CAMPGROUND RATINGS

Beauty:	★★★★
Site privacy:	★★★
Site spaciousness:	★★★★★
Quiet:	★★★★
Security:	★★★★★
Cleanliness/upkeep:	★★★★

Kentucky's best camping in the "Far West" sits on a bluff overlooking the Mississippi River.

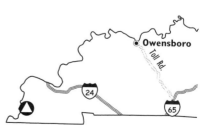

WESTERN

Otherwise, the well-separated sites are all good. Top out on the hill and come to 10 of the best sites—those that overlook the river. These are obviously the most desirable spots, and they even have little viewing benches between them and the river bluff. Campers can see far into the Show Me State. Turn away from the bluff and drop down a bit, reaching more heavily shaded sites to complete the loop.

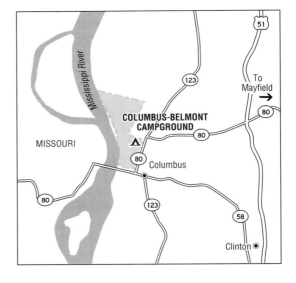

In the center of the loop lies a building with laundry, showers, a playground, and camp office. Since the campground has water and electricity, there will be RVs. But the good camping here is worth a little face time with the big rig set. A view from here or the park picnic area will help you understand why the location of this state park was known during the Civil War as the "Gibraltar of the West." The Union thought if it could get below here on the Mississippi River, it could work on splitting the Confederacy in two. But first it had to get past Columbus. The Confederates built earthworks on the bluffs, which you can see today via 2.5 miles of self-guided trails. These earthen fortification held cannons that fired upon Federal ships to slow boat traffic. Johnny Reb also laid a huge, mile-long metal chain across the river to further impede traffic. This chain is on display at the park's museum.

Gen. U.S. Grant attacked the town of Belmont, across the river in Missouri. In the resulting battle, over 1,000 lives were lost, yet neither side was able to claim victory. However, the South was outflanked and later abandoned the fort atop the bluff on the Kentucky side.

Today, the tranquillity beneath the big trees atop this bluff belies the battle of yesteryear. I sat upon a park bench one fine spring afternoon, looking out on the seemingly small boats plying the Mississippi below. Nearby was a cannon from the battle, discovered and subsequently restored in 1998. Later, I took a walk to see more history, imagining the men who occupied the Confederate trenches back in 1862. It's ironic that the catastrophic flood in 1927, which wiped out an entire town, could lead to the preservation of this historic park. Columbus-Belmont preserves history and today offers an escape from the rigors of daily life underneath the big trees.

Supplies can be had in nearby Columbus. Remember that even though the campground is open year-round, some of the other park facilities, such as the museum, are only open April through October.

KEY INFORMATION

Columbus-Belmont State Park
P.O. Box 9
Columbus, KY 42032

Operated by: Kentucky State Parks

Information: (270) 677-2327, www.kystateparks.com

Open: Year-round

Individual sites: 38

Each site has: Picnic table, fire ring, water, electricity

Site assignment: First come, first served; no reservation

Registration: At camp office

Facilities: Hot shower, flush toilets, laundry

Parking: At campsites only

Fee: $14 per night

Elevation: 450 feet

Restrictions:

Pets—On 6-foot leash only

Fires—In fire rings only

Alcoholic beverages—Not allowed

Vehicles—None

Other—14-day stay limit

To get there: From exit 22 on the Purchase Parkway near Mayfield, head west on KY 80 for 28 miles to Cheatham Street in Columbus. Turn right on Cheatham Street and follow it one mile to dead-end at the park.

D O G   C R E E K

Munfordville

We can only speculate how Dog Creek got its name. Maybe a dog was lost or found or born here, way back when. We do know the Army Corps of Engineers named this campground after the nearby stream, Dog Creek, which flows into Nolin Lake, an impoundment of the Nolin River. The name Nolin comes from early area settlers. The settlers were overnighting on the river, and a young girl named Lynn wandered away from the riverside camp and became lost. Other members of the group looked for her but to no avail, returning to camp day after day, uttering the words, "No Lynn," giving the river and later the lake their names. The father, after giving up on Lynn, died of a broken heart. You will not want to wander away from Dog Creek Campground, with its many lakeside sites overlooking Nolin Lake, but you may get lost in a world of fun and relaxation.

Dog Creek Campground is located on the Dog Creek arm of the impoundment. Pass the campground entrance station and a pond to your right, and then enter Area A. At the front are a few primitive sites that are too open to the sun. Come alongside the swim area and some partially shaded campsites alongside the shore. Some of the sites away from the shore are more open. For those making reservations, consider sites 6, 9, 11, and 13. Campers can pull their boats directly up to these sites. The loop climbs a hill and comes to 10 sites with

CAMPGROUND RATINGS

Beauty: ★★★★
Site privacy: ★★★
Site spaciousness: ★★★
Quiet: ★★★
Security: ★★★★★
Cleanliness/upkeep: ★★★★

Dog Creek offers the best tent camping on Nolin Lake.

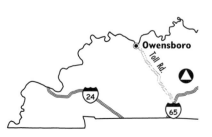

WESTERN

electrical hookups. The big rigs park here. At this point, you meet up with Area B loop, which loops back out toward the lake. As with Area A, you'll find wide-open primitive sites at the beginning of this loop, too. Area B's electric sites are on the same hill as Area A's sites. These hill sites are well shaded by pine and cedar, but they aren't on the lake and are a little cramped. Starting with campsite 16, the waterside sites go on to 24, overlooking the clear and green water of the lake

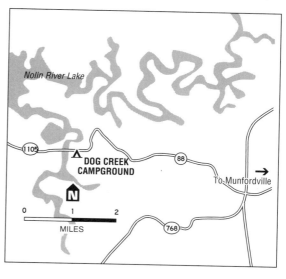

backed by wooded hills and occasional limestone bluffs. Landscaping timbers are used to level these waterside campsites that are well spread apart. Area C is the smallest of the bunch, located under a tall grove of pines. Shade lovers will prefer these sites. A few lakeside sites are here, too. Campsites 10 and 11 are the best waterside sites in Area C. Overall, campsite spaciousness depends on the campsite, and campsite privacy is limited by an understory mostly of grass.

The swim beach is a big attraction on hot summer days. A boat launch is adjacent to the campground, as is a playground and picnic area. Dog Creek is popular with boaters who launch their boat and then park it near their water-side campsite. Those without boats can still enjoy the campground, with its swim beach and lake views. If you are interested, boats can be rented at Wax Recreation Area, just a few miles north of Dog Creek. Anglers vie for bass, bream, and catfish swimming beneath the water. Corps rangers conduct programs on summer weekends for kids and adults. Also nearby is Nolin Lake State Park, which has water recreation opportunities and nature trails. Learn more about the lake at the Nolin Lake Army Corps of Engineers office, and check out the dam and spillway of this body of water impounded in 1963. Mammoth Cave National Park is just an hour away to the south.

Pick up your supplies in Munfordville, as there are not many nearby stores. Dog Creek will fill on summer holiday weekends. But campers need not worry about not getting a campsite, since sites can be reserved. Just make sure when you come here not to get lost, like Lynn did.

To get there: From exit 65 on I-65, take US 31W just a short distance to downtown Munfordville to KY 88. Turn right on KY 88 and follow it west, passing under I-65 along the 17 miles to Hart County 1015. Turn left on 1015 and follow it 0.9 mile to the campground entrance on your right.

ENERGY LAKE

Lake City

Energy Lake is an ideal example of enhancing natural resources to create a better recreation area. Start with a rolling shoreline on a scenic body of water. Integrate a just-the-right-size campground into the landscape (read: 48 campsites spread over four loops). Add a few amenities, but keep its rustic feel (read: camping shelters). Locate it where there are activities right at the campground with others nearby (read: the Nature Station). What you end up with is a complete tent camping package (read: come here).

Cross the dam that separates Energy Lake from Lake Barkley to enter the campground. Pass the entrance station and climb a hill to Area A. The 12 sites are attractively set on a high peninsula and leveled with landscaping timbers. Seven of the sites overlook the lake, which is 60 feet below, offering a watery panorama. The camping pads are large and well spaced, but they don't have too much of an understory between them. A fully equipped bathhouse lies in the center of Area A, as in all four loops. It also has two of the unusual camping shelters. Tent campers use these three-sided shelters, with a picnic table inside, during rainy times to cook or just hang out. And that can help a lot when the weather is bad. However, you can't just set your gear up and sleep in here, so keep your bedding in your tent.

CAMPGROUND RATINGS

Beauty:	★★★★★
Site privacy:	★★★
Site spaciousness:	★★★★
Quiet:	★★★★
Security:	★★★★★
Cleanliness/upkeep:	★★★★★

The rainy-day camping shelters here are just one reason to stay at Energy Lake.

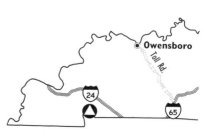

WESTERN

There will be a mix of RVs and tents at Energy Lake, but Area B, with only two electric sites, is the sole domain of the canvas set. This loop is the only one away from the lake, and it heads higher up the hill. The sites are spacious, resting beneath a hickory-oak woodland. Two camping shelters and two water spigots make life a little more comfortable.

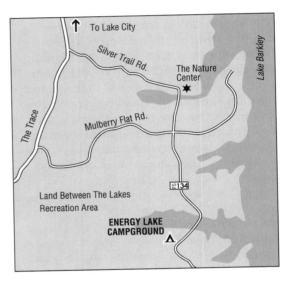

Pass the day use area, which is down a steep road leading to a grassy flat. A swim beach and play area, with a court, small ball field, and a horseshoe pit are located here. Come to Area C, one of the most unusual loops I have ever seen. Drop down a hill, passing some large sites and come to a lakeside site. The loop road then makes a figure-eight, with three good lakeside sites. Turn away from the lake, where four more good campsites are located. Area D is farther down the main campground road. The road drops so steeply that you reckon an elevator would better serve the tiered campsites beside the road. Make no mistake, the sites themselves are level and attractive. It is the road that is scary. A couple of campsite shelters are here, too, as well as some more lakeview sites. The rest of the sites are away from the water.

All campsites can be reserved up to 11 months in advance, so if you want to start relaxing early, phone in that reservation, then cruise on to Energy Lake. I recommend reservations on summer weekends. Bring your boat to enjoy the 370-acre impoundment or nearby Lake Barkely, which is just across the dam road over which you drove. If you don't have a boat, rent a canoe here. Many folks paddle for fun or cast their rod for crappie, catfish, or bass. Two loop trails totaling over six miles can be accessed right from your campsite. They wind and roll all over this hilly country.

What makes a trip to Energy Lake really special is the nearby Nature Station. It offers environmental education in an attractive setting. The Learning Center has exhibits on the wildlife of Land Between the Lakes. The Backyard has plants native to this region, along with stray or injured animals that have been taken in by the Nature Station. There are also aquatic creatures in the turtle and fish ponds. You can see a bald eagle, owls, bobcats, coyotes, deer, and more. Kids can really have a good time, and the adults might learn a thing or two themselves. Outside the Nature Station is another set of trails. The Center Furnace Trail checks out the remnants of a great iron furnace and the iron industry of this area. The Hematite and Honker trails circle small lakes, offering possibilities of seeing waterfowl. You can also rent canoes to paddle Honker Lake. Grab your friends and family to enjoy the natural side of the LBL at Energy Lake.

To get there: From exit 31 on I-24 near Lake City, head south on KY 453 for 7 miles to intersect the Trace. Keep south on the Trace for 9 miles to Silver Trail Road. Turn left on Silver Trail Road and follow it for 3 miles to paved Forest Road 134, near the Nature Station. Turn right on FR 134 and follow it for 4.7 miles to reach Energy Lake.

KEY INFORMATION

Energy Lake
100 Van Morgan Drive
Golden Pond, KY 42211

Operated by: United States Forest Service

Information: (270) 924-2000; www.lbl.org; reservations (270) 924-3044

Open: March through October

Individual sites: 35 electric; 13 nonelectric

Each site has: Picnic table, fire ring

Site assignment: First come, first served, and by reservation

Registration: At campground entrance station

Facilities: Hot showers, flush toilets, phone, ice machine

Parking: At campsites only

Fee: $12 per night spring, fall, $13 per night summer; $3 per night electricity

Elevation: 360 feet

Restrictions:

Pets—On 6-foot leash only

Fires—In fire rings only

Alcoholic beverages—At campsites only

Vehicles—None

Other—21-day stay-limit

HOUCHINS FERRY

Brownsville

Mammoth Cave National Park contains the most extensive known cave system on earth. It has to be seen to be comprehended. There are above-ground attractions as well, like a surface trail system that traverses the largest protected natural area in Western Kentucky. And there are the rivers, the Nolin and the Green, that offer recreation opportunities of their own. And it is on the Green River that Houchins Ferry campground lies, which is the starting point for tent campers who come to enjoy this national treasure.

The park's windy road keeps the big rigs away and makes Houchins Ferry exclusive tent camper territory. At the end of this road is a ferry, which takes cars one at a time across the Green River. The campground is near the ferry, past the water spigot and screened vault toilets, and stretches out along a flat about 30 feet above the Green River. Hardwoods shade the entire camping area, which is backed by a steep hill rising away from the Green. The understory is open and grassy. The initial eight sites are directly riverside. The first site is right by the ferry and is shaded by a large sycamore. The next couple of sites are a little close together, then become more spread apart. Landscaping timbers delineate each campsite. Come to a small auto turnaround, where a couple more campsites are situated and have the best privacy. The final two campsites are away from the river and are

CAMPGROUND RATINGS

Beauty:	★★★★
Site privacy:	★★★
Site spaciousness:	★★★★
Quiet:	★★★★
Security:	★★★★
Cleanliness/upkeep:	★★★★

Houchins Ferry is the ideal base camp for both above and below ground attractions at Mammoth Cave National Park.

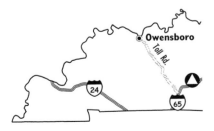

WESTERN

well distanced from one another. Across from the campground is a brick picnic shelter with two fireplaces, which could come in handy on rainy days.

Touring Mammoth Cave is a must. There is nothing I can say that will match the actual grandeur of this World Heritage Site. There are tours of all types, depending on your stamina and fortitude. The rougher ones are best, as the groups are smaller and explore more remote parts of the cave. The cave and park visitor center are 15 miles

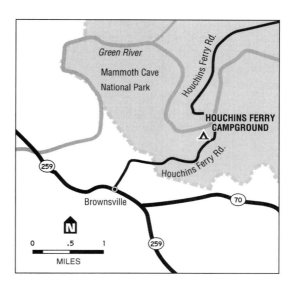

distant from Houchins Ferry. I recommend arriving at the campground, and making a cave tour reservation for the next day by calling the park number. That way you can be guaranteed a spot on the next day's tour. Then spend your first day enjoying the above ground features of this national park. Just across the Green River is a 60-mile trail system that will surprise even jaded hikers. These paths roll past rivers, steep bluffs, sinkholes, waterfall and old homesites. The McCoy Hollow Trail is underused and under appreciated. Drop down off Temple Hill and come alongside the Green River, passing a big rockhouse and the Three Springs area. Wind in and out of little valleys to a decent view from the McCoy Hollow campsite. The Wet Prong Loop is a great springtime wild-flower walk. Blue Springs is a scenic spot along this circuit. Head over Good Spring Church, preserved from the pioneer days and make the Good Springs Loop. The waterfall at the Waterfall campsite makes for a good cooling- off spot. You will be surprised at the ruggedness of the overall terrain. This ten-mile loop is an all-day affair.

If watery adventures are your idea of fun, try the Green River. A 26-mile portion of the river flows through the national park. You can take a ride on a tour boat that departs near the park visitor center. Or you can paddle a canoe on your own. Several outfitters are listed on the campground information board. One 12-mile trip down this river, which is really green, starts at Green River Ferry and ends at Houchins Ferry. The current moves pretty quick, but there are no hazardous rapids. The scenery here rivals that of the trail system. Anglers can vie for bass, crappie, and bluegill. No state fishing license is needed. However, you must comply with Kentucky creel limits. This may be the only limit to your enjoyment of Mammoth Cave National Park.

To get there: From KY 70 in Brownsville, take Houchins Ferry Road 1.8 miles north to the campground, which is on the Green River.

KEY INFORMATION

Houchins Ford
Mammoth Cave National Park
Mammoth Cave, KY 42259

Operated by: National Park Service

Information: (270) 758-2328, www.nps.gov/maca

Open: March–November

Individual sites: 12

Each site has: Picnic table, fire grate, lantern post with additional mini-table

Site assignment: First come, first served; no reservation

Registration: Self-registration on site

Facilities: Water spigot, vault toilet

Parking: At campsites only

Fee: $10 per night

Elevation: 420 feet

Restrictions:

Pets—On 6-foot leash only

Fires—In fire rings only

Alcoholic beverages—At campsites only

Vehicles—Not suitable for large trailers or RVs

Other—14-day stay limit

LAKE MALONE STATE PARK

Central City

Lake Malone is a small state park. However, it makes the most of its small size. The setting here helps. Some may argue this point, but Lake Malone may be the Bluegrass State's most attractive impoundment. I spent a Sunday afternoon in spring relaxing on its shores, with the bright sun warming my bones. The wind was gently lapping waves on the steep shoreline. Boaters were cruising the clear water framed by 200-foot sandstone cliffs. Families fished from the banks, while a young boy played with his puppy. An older couple grilled hamburgers by the picnic shelter. In other words, it was one of those idyllic tent camping days you dream of during those long winter nights.

The two park campgrounds aren't idyllic, but they will more than do. The main campground is small, like the state park. It makes a small loop beneath a mix of tulip, oak, and maple trees. Most campsites radiate outward from the hilltop center of the campground, but they are kept level with landscaping timbers. Some of the sites have obscured views of Lake Malone. The sites in the center of the loop are too open to the sun, have no privacy, and are generally undesirable. Since the main campground has water and electricity, the big rigs like it, though a stray tent camper or two will overnight here. Pass the fully equipped bathhouse and cross a field large enough for the University of Kentucky

CAMPGROUND RATINGS

Beauty:	★★★
Site privacy:	★★★
Site spaciousness:	★★★★★
Quiet:	★★★★
Security:	★★★★
Cleanliness/upkeep:	★★★★

The bluffs of Lake Malone and primitive campsites make a great camping combination.

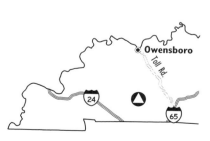

WESTERN

and the University of Tennessee to play a football game. Future sports stars will be frolicking here with footballs and Frisbees. There is also a more conventional playground by the field. Just past here is the primitive camping area, where tent campers will find a site. And there are plenty. The park brochure boasts the park has over 100 sites, which might be a little generous. The 40 picnic tables and grills set beneath a mix of tall pine trees and hardwoods are situated in a hodgepodge fashion with no marked or numbered sites. Just pull your vehicle up to the spot you desire and pitch your tent. Campsite spaciousness is at its maximum here. When the other campgrounds are filling on summer holiday weekends, come to Lake Malone. You will never be turned away for lack of a campsite. Park personnel told me that if the primitive area somehow fills, you could camp in the field. However, the main campground will fill before the holiday weekend starts.

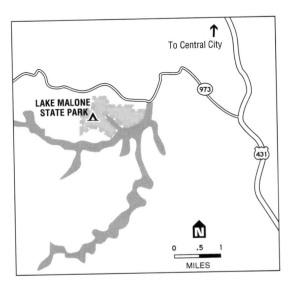

The swim beach and state park marina are not directly accessible from the campground. This is a double-edged sword: the lack of direct access keeps the campground quieter, but campers have to get in their car to reach the beach, which is open from Memorial Day to Labor Day. This swim beach looks down on the attractive lake. Parents will be happy to know a lifeguard is on duty. The small park marina stands alongside the swim beach, where boats will launch in search of channel catfish, crappie, and bass. Others will pleasure boat on the 788-acre Lake Malone. If you are boatless, you can rent pontoon, fishing, and pedal boats to see this pretty lake. For hiking, the Laurel Trail is directly accessible from the campground. Walk down to the picnic area and pick up the path, which runs for 1.5 miles along the lake, passing rock shelters and native flora of Kentucky. Supplies can be had at a general store just outside the park entrance. I hope the weather will be as fine for you as it was for me on my trip to Lake Malone.

To get there: From exit 58 on Wendell H. Ford Parkway near Central City, head south on US 431 for 21 miles to KY 973. Turn right on KY 973 and follow it for 4 miles to the state park, on your left. The campground is at the second entrance to the state park, coming from US 431.

KEY INFORMATION

Lake Malone State Park
P.O. Box 93,
** 331 State Route Road 8001**
Dunmore, KY 42339

Operated by: Kentucky State Parks

Information: (270) 657-2111, www.kystateparks.com

Open: Year-round

Individual sites: 60

Each site has: Main Campground has picnic table, fire ring, lantern post, water, electricity; Primitive Campground has picnic table, fire ring

Site assignment: First come, first served; no reservation

Registration: At campground ranger station

Facilities: Hot showers, water spigots

Parking: At campsites only

Fee: $14 per night Main Campground; $8.50 per night Primitive Campground

Elevation: 600 feet

Restrictions:

Pets—On 6-foot leash only

Fires—In fire rings only

Alcoholic beverages—Not allowed

Vehicles—None

Other—14-day stay limit

PENNYRILE FOREST STATE PARK

Dawson Springs

The first "camper" at Pennyrile Forest was a fellow named John Thompson. He had traveled west from Virginia way back in 1808, looking for a new place to homestead. He pushed over the Cumberland Gap, across the Great Wilderness and onward, eventually making it to what is now known as the Tradewater River (you cross it on the way in from Dawson Springs). Winter was approaching, so ol' John decided to house himself and his family under a big rock shelter, located on park grounds. He lived for over a year under the rock and then settled down for good in a house he built, with a few families joining him in later years. As decades passed, much of the area farmland became worn out. The Commonwealth of Kentucky acquired the park in the 1940s and has managed the 15,000 acres as a state forest and park ever since. I can't say for sure, but I think John Thompson would like the family campground and the activities that now take place in and around the hollow where he settled. Just bring your tent so you won't have to camp under a rock.

The campground has plenty of sites, but it's not too big. Pass the combination campstore and registration station. It is open Wednesday through Sunday during the warm season. Pass a loop on your left. Numerically this is the last loop. A shaded miniature golf course is on the right. Come to the first loop on the right, just beyond

CAMPGROUND RATINGS

Beauty:	★★★★
Site privacy:	★★★
Site spaciousness:	★★★★
Quiet:	★★★★
Security:	★★★★
Cleanliness/upkeep:	★★★★★

This state park and forest is great in size and beauty.

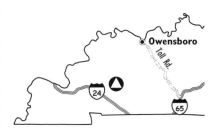

WESTERN

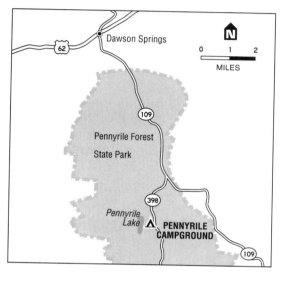

the course. Large sites are both in the shade and sun and circle around a fully equipped bathhouse. The slope of the paved auto pull-ins keeps RVs away. Enter the main camping road, which has campsites on both side of it on a more level area. Attractive tall pine trees with a few dogwoods shade the camping area. Grass grows around the large gravel camping pads. The pines give way to deciduous trees at a small auto turnaround with large, level sites that are the camping area's finest. The final loop, near the campground entrance, is the least popular. It is also the most hilly, with many less-than-level sites. Solitude seekers will be fine under the tall pines here. The campground rarely fills, save for summer holiday weekends.

For nearby fun, in addition to the miniature golf which is lighted for night play, there is Pennyrile Lake. Campers can easily walk down to the water. There is a scenic swim beach here, set in a cove against a tall stone bluff. The 56-acre lake also holds a few fish, namely bass, bluegill, and catfish. During the warm season, campers can rent rowboats, paddleboats, and trolling motors to get around this quiet impoundment and try their luck. There is also a canoe rental outfit near Dawson Springs for those who want to float the Tradewater River.

The state forest surrounds the state park. For hikers and bikers there is no appreciable distinction between the park and forest. But know this: hikers have 23 miles of trails to walk, and there is an additional set of mountain biking routes ranging from 2 to 19 miles in length. The hiking trails near the campground pass rockhouses (similar to what Thompson used), circle the lake, cruise along creeks, and meander through rich woods. The Macedonia Trail is in the state forest and offers loops from one to five miles in length. Grab a map at the registration station. If you need to get supplies not found at the park, just walk the Pennyrile Nature Trail. This path goes for 13 miles back to Dawson Springs. Of course, that would make it a 26-mile round trip, with supplies on your back. On second thought, you'd better take the car.

To get there: From exit 24 on the Wendell H. Ford Parkway near Dawson Springs, head south on Kentucky 109 for 10 miles to KY 398. Turn right on KY 398 and follow it for 2 miles to enter the park.

TAILWATER

Bowling Green

It was a summer weekend, and I was determined to go tent camping. The thermometer hovered around 90°, so water was a necessary feature of any campground. I just couldn't decide between a lake or river, so I headed to Tailwater campground on Barren River Lake, where there was a little bit of both. Tailwater is a quiet campground with a relaxed pace, but it also offers plenty of action for those who want some. It lies along the tailwater of the Barren River Dam, which is in sight of the campground. Barren River Lake is just on the other side of the dam.

The river's name comes from early settlers of the region. Indians had kept the area around the Barren River burned off, forming grasslands that attracted game for them to hunt. This lack of trees in the great Kentucky forests of the time made the area seem barren, and the name stuck. After a night at Tailwater, you may be sticking around for a few more nights.

Drive beyond the dam stilling basin (read: outflow of water from a concrete tunnel beneath the dam) and come to the campground. Pass the entrance station and approach the first set of sites, located on a bluff overlooking the stilling basin and the Barren River. The road lies between the river and the campsites, save for one direct riverside site. These shady large sites are appealing nonetheless. The road turns, leading to riverside campsites

CAMPGROUND RATINGS

Beauty:	★★★★
Site privacy:	★★★★
Site spaciousness:	★★★
Quiet:	★★★
Security:	★★★★★
Cleanliness/upkeep:	★★★★

This campground offers a variety of environments near Barren River Lake.

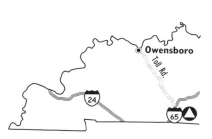

WESTERN

beneath maple, sweetgum, and other hardwoods. Grass forms the main understory.

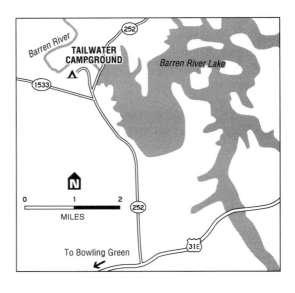

Near campsite 22, you'll see an interesting contraption. A metal cable has been strung across the river; attached to it is a box used to carry folks across the river if they become stranded on the far side. This is for emergency use only. You'll see a few more campsites set along the river bluff before reaching the campground boat ramp. Beyond here is another string of shady sites that overlook the clear, green Barren River. You'll come to a gravel auto turnaround and two campsites away from the river. A full-time campground attendant makes for a safe and enjoyable stay. Tailwater rarely fills, even on holiday weekends, but to assure yourself a spot, just call the reservation line.

A large grassy area runs parallel to the campground road. Here is a softball field, a play area, horseshoe pits, campground amphitheater, and a new bathhouse with hot showers. There are also a couple of cold showers open to the sun and the world. Keep your clothes on if you get under these nozzles.

This is an angler's campground. Folks fish at the stilling basin, going for big striped bass. But there are other fish in these bone-chilling cold waters, such as periodically stocked trout. Bass and catfish can also be caught. Most folks bank-fish from the river's edge along the campground. Being on the river keeps most boaters away, but there is a boat ramp for those inclined. Boaters can also head up to Peninsula Recreation Area on Barren River Lake for some lake boating in warmer waters. Swimming is not allowed at Tailwater Campground, due to the super-cold water coming from below the dam and the fact that water releases from the dam may catch swimmers unawares. So do like I did and just make the short drive to Quarry Recreation Area, less than a mile distant, to enjoy the swim beach there. Fishing piers are also located at Quarry. While heading that way, stop at the dam overlook, where you can peer down on Tailwater Campground and over at the scenic lake.

If the fish aren't biting, try a hike. A scout-built trail leaves the campground and makes a loop into the woods, crossing wood bridges and a wildlife viewing area. When you do come to Tailwater, make sure and explore not only this trail, but also Barren River Lake. It is a very attractive place, with plenty of water for a cooling dip on a hot summer day.

KEY INFORMATION

Tailwater Campground
11088 Finney Road
Glasgow, KY 42141

Operated by: U.S. Army Corps of Engineers

Information: (270) 646-2055; www.lrl.usace.army.mil/brl; reservations (877) 444-6777

Open: Year-round

Individual sites: 48

Each site has: Picnic table, fire grate, lantern post, cooking table

Site assignment: First come, first served and by reservation

Registration: At campground registration station

Facilities: Hot showers, flush toilets, water spigots

Parking: At campsites only

Fee: $11 per night

Elevation: 500 feet

Restrictions:

Pets—On 6-foot leash only

Fires—In fire rings only

Alcoholic beverages—At campsites only

Vehicles—Maximum 6 campers per site

Other—14-day stay limit

To get there: From exit 22 on I-65 near Bowling Green, head south on US 231 for 18 miles to US 31E. Turn left on US 31E and follow it for 8.2 miles north to KY 252. Turn left on 252 and follow it 4.1 miles to Tailwater Campground, which will be on your left. If you cross the Barren River Lake Dam, you have gone too far.

CENTRAL
KENTUCKY

BEE ROCK

Somerset

Vacationers have been coming to Bee Rock for a couple of hundred years to get away from it all. In the early 1800s, Sublimity Spring Resort Hotel stood where the campground now lies. Columbus Graham, a hero in the War of 1812, ran the resort, which offered an escape from malaria, yellow fever, and other plagues of the lower South. It was described as "an Eden for children, a sanitarium for invalids, a paradise for lovers, and a haven of rest for the tired." How does that sound?

Bee Rock Campground may not cure anything, but it is an attractive respite for tent campers. The cliff known as Bee Rock got its name from the population of wild bees living inside its hollow interior. Tired of the "wild" bees getting into their hives, local beekeepers destroyed the hollow part of the cliff with dynamite. Legend has it that so much honey flowed that it reached the Rockcastle River. Not to worry—a great view remains of the rocks and cliff along the Rockcastle River at Bee Rock via foot trails that start right at the campground. The Rockcastle River also offers fishing and boating.

The Rockcastle divides the campground. Coming from the east, you will first reach the smaller East Side Campground, comprised entirely of walk-in tent sites. The dead-end access road leads to roadside parking areas for the tent sites. Each site is up the hill away from the river. Past these

CAMPGROUND RATINGS

Beauty:	★★★★
Site privacy:	★★★★
Site spaciousness:	★★★
Quiet:	★★★★
Security:	★★★
Cleanliness/upkeep:	★★★★

Bee Rock has been a getaway for travelers since the early 1800s.

CENTRAL

sites are new vault toilets and the Sublimity Bridge, built by the Civilian Conservation Corps in the 1930s. More good sites lie up the hill. These sites are all far from one another and are heavily wooded.

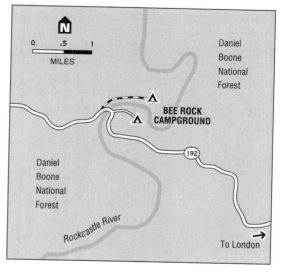

The West Side Campground road passes Sublimity Bridge to enter the camping area. Come to a solo site alongside the river, then swing around a hollow, passing one end of the Bee Rock Loop Trail and newer vault toilets. Other shady lakeside sites lie along the Rockcastle. The understory is limited, cutting down on campsite privacy. The sites are generally spacious. Pop-up trailers often occupy some of the larger sites.

Come to an auto turnaround and notice the large boulders that add natural landscaping. Of special note is site 15, which is surrounded by many of these gray boulders, adding a special touch. The sites away from the river are more heavily wooded and less popular. Water spigots are located throughout the campground.

Local campers favor Bee Rock, which is a good sign. Campers can generally find a site anytime, especially in the East Side Campground. Many folks come to get a little relaxation (like that touted back in the 1800s). Other campers will be seen bank-fishing for bass, bream, and catfish. There is a boat launch here, for this campground stands at the uppermost reach of Lake Cumberland. Upstream of here the Rockcastle flows free as a designated Kentucky Wild River. You can explore it via the Rockcastle Narrows Trail. The path starts near the boat ramp and follows the Rockcastle upstream past Cane Creek. Here, hikers leave left to reach the Narrows, some of the most challenging whitewater in Kentucky. To the right is the Winding Stair Gap Trail, which passes wildlife clearings and the foundation of the old resort hotel.

You can also reach the Narrows from the west side of the Rockcastle via Trail #503 (Rockcastle Narrows West Trail). It allows hikers to reach secluded fishing spots before it turns away from the river and connects to the "must do" path of Bee Rock, the Bee Rock Loop. The Bee Rock Loop climbs steeply to a scenic view of the Rockcastle River, then circles around back to the campground. Maybe after a good look around at the scenery of the Rockcastle valley you may understand why folks have been coming here for all these years.

> **To get there:** From exit 38 on I-75 near London, head west on KY 192 for 18 miles to the bridge over the Rockcastle River. The campground is on both sides of the river.

KEY INFORMATION

Bee Rock
135 Realty Lane
Somerset, KY 42501

Operated by: U.S. Forest Service

Information: (606) 679-2010, www.southernregion.fs.fed. us/boone

Open: East Side year-round; West Side April–October

Individual sites: 8 walk-in tent sites; 18 tent/trailer sites

Each site has: Picnic table, fire ring, lantern post, tent pad

Site assignment: First come, first served; no reservation

Registration: Self-registration on site

Facilities: Water spigots, vault toilets

Parking: At campsites only

Fee: $5 per night

Elevation: 730 feet

Restrictions:

Pets—On 6-foot leash only

Fires—In fire rings only

Alcoholic beverages—At campsites only

Vehicles—Maximum 2 vehicles per site

Other—14-day stay limit

FORT BOONESBOROUGH

Winchester

Consider this: thanks to numerous twists of fate, you can actually camp where Daniel Boone camped should you stay the night at Fort Boonesborough State Park. See, when ol' Dan'l set out over the Cumberland Gap from Tennessee to make a settlement, he chose the banks of the Kentucky River to build his town. Specifically, he spied out Sycamore Flats, the primitive camping area at what is now the state park, to use as his fort and out of which the town would grow. However, before he could get started, one of his comrades persuaded Boone to locate the fort on higher ground adjacent to Sycamore Flats. Fort Boonesborough was eventually abandoned as settlers went on to greener pastures. In the early 1900s, a fellow bought the property, and later, his son donated it to Kentucky, which developed the state park where Daniel and company laid their heads.

The main campground rests above Sycamore Flats. Several rows of RV spaces lie in an open, sun-whipped plain. The 167 sites remind me of an RV dealership where I wouldn't want my worst enemy to camp. I wonder what Daniel Boone would have thought of this? The redeeming values of this area are the bathhouses and the ranger's meeting room, where there are indoor games for rainy days. Drive past the main campground and veer right, dropping down into Sycamore Flats. True

CAMPGROUND RATINGS

Beauty:	★★★
Site privacy:	★★★
Site spaciousness:	★★★★
Quiet:	★★★
Security:	★★★★★
Cleanliness/upkeep:	★★★★

Pitch your tent where Daniel Boone did back in 1775.

CENTRAL

to its name, huge sycamore trees shade the camping area, along with maples. Grass grows in places where the sun reaches the ground. Two small creeks bisect the flat. The sites are located in a hodgepodge fashion. I hope Daniel's outfit was more organized than the primitive camping area. To the right are some popular sites before the campground road splits. The road to the right runs alongside a small creek and comes to some sites open to sun and shade. It ends in a small loop near the campground check-in station.

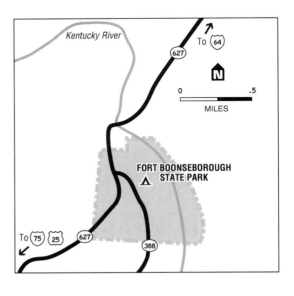

The other road crosses a bridge and reaches more scattered sites. One thing Daniel's cohort was right about was the penchant for Sycamore Flats to flood. The threat back in 1775 was from the Kentucky River exceeding its banks. Today, a dam lies just upstream of the campground, eliminating that worry. However, the flats can become muddy after rains, making some of the camp-sites less than desirable. The primitive area rarely fills up, save for summer holiday weekends. A camp store is located near the entrance for convenience.

While the original fort that began in Sycamore Flats is no longer here, a replica lies within walking distance of the campground. You can tour this replica, which follows the actual design of the original. Militia reenactments, rustic living skills, and old-time ways are demonstrated year-round. This will give you an idea what times were like then. Add to that the idea of hostile Indians outside the fort walls that didn't want you around.

The best way to access the fort is by way of the Pioneer Forage Trail. Back in 1775, camp stores or chain stores didn't exist, and the settlers had to get what they could from the land. Along the way, plants and trees used for food and shelter are marked. This 0.8-mile trail starts near the campground entrance. Another interesting path is the Kentucky River-walk Trail; it keeps to the valley of the river, passing by natural, human, and geologic features. Also along the banks of the Kentucky River is a swim beach upstream of the campground near the dam. If you prefer chlorinated water, swim in the large, modern pool, open from Memorial Day to Labor Day. Anglers can bank-fish the river or use the park boat ramp to launch their craft.

Park programs are held every weekend to keep child and adult campers busy learning more about the human and natural history of Kentucky. The park and its programs are a continual reminder that Daniel Boone paved the way for all of us to enjoy the beauty of this area.

To get there: From exit 94 on I-64 near Winchester, head south on KY 627 South Truck/KY 1958 for 3 miles to KY 627. Turn right on KY 627 South and follow it for 7 miles to KY 388 South. Turn left on KY 388 and follow it a short distance to the campground, which will be on your left.

KEY INFORMATION

Fort Boonesborough
4375 Boonesborough Road
Richmond, KY 40475

Operated by: Kentucky State Parks

Information: (859) 527-3131, www.kystateparks.com

Open: Year-round

Individual sites: 30 primitive, 167 water and electric

Each site has: Primitive has picnic table, fire ring; others have water electricity

Site assignment: First come, first served; no reservation

Registration: At campground entrance booth

Facilities: Hot showers, flush toilets, laundry, pay phone, camp store

Parking: At campsites only

Fee: $8.50 per night primitive; $16 per night other

Elevation: 600 feet

Restrictions:

Pets—On 6-foot leash only

Fires—In fire rings only

Alcoholic beverages—Not allowed

Vehicles—None

Other—14-day stay limit

GREAT MEADOW

Williamsburg

Great Meadows campground lies deep in the valley of Rock Creek, a Wild and Scenic River that cuts between nearby Laurel Ridge and Backbone Ridge. Visitors that camp along the river's banks can drop a line to taunt the local fish or hike in Daniel Boone National Forest and adjacent Big South Fork National River Recreation Area, where arches and great overlooks await discovery. Great Meadow lies at the end of the road, which has its advantages, including little to no auto traffic and great overall solitude.

Great Meadow Campground is divided into two separate loops. As you head up the Rock Creek Valley on the dead-end road, you'll come first to Deer Loop. This loop offers above-par campsite privacy. Three of the eight campsites are inside this loop—a grassy field with scattered white pines. Vault toilets, a water spigot, and a horseshoe pit are located here. The campsites on the outside of the loop are heavily wooded in white pine, oak, hemlock, sycamore, and hickory, and they are backed against a high ridge. A couple of them are double sites.

Just a hundred or so yards further on the left-hand side of the road is the Raccoon Loop. This six-site year-round loop lies directly on Rock Creek. The center of the loop is mostly open and grassy, adding an airy atmosphere to the heavily wooded valley. There is not as much vegetation

CAMPGROUND RATINGS

Beauty:	★★★★
Site privacy:	★★★★
Site spaciousness:	★★★★★
Quiet:	★★★★★
Security:	★★★
Cleanliness/upkeep:	★★★★

Great Meadow offers great tent camping as well as great hiking and fishing in the most southwesterly section of the Daniel Boone National Forest.

CENTRAL

between campsites, making for less site privacy than in Deer Loop. However, the campsites are widely separated. A horseshoe pit, two newer-style vault toilets, and a water spigot serve this loop.

Once on the loop, come to a tiered campsite overlooking the water immediately on the right, located beside a large rock beneath a white pine tree. The next site is riverside site. A rock wall from settler days is visible across the creek. Water lovers will favor the third

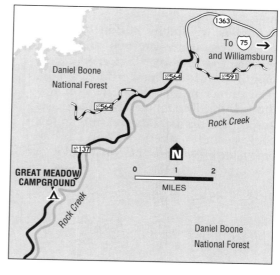

site, as it lies adjacent to a pool backed up by rocks in the stream. The fourth site is also on the water. Come to an auto turnaround and a wooded site off the water and far from the others. A final site lies adjacent to the field away from Rock Creek. Great Meadows will fill on summer weekends and holidays, so get there as early as you can.

Just across Rock Creek is Kentucky's premier trail, the Sheltowee Trace. It is your pathway to the natural attractions in the Rock Creek Valley. There is no direct access from the campground, so you must cross the creek to reach the trail, then proceed up the valley or down, depending on your whim. Upstream is the Parker Mountain Trail, also accessible by car at the very end of the dead-end road (the Rock Creek trailhead). This trail leads west up to Buffalo Arch on the Tennessee-Kentucky line. It's 2.5 miles one way. Another option at the Rock Creek trailhead is a 7.5-mile loop hike over footbridges and past waterfalls, rock houses, and an old pioneer cemetery. Take the Sheltowee Trace up along Rock Creek to the Coffee Trail, then head back north on the Rock Creek Loop Trail down along Massey Branch and back to the trailhead.

Another great hike starts at the Hemlock Grove parking area, two miles downstream from the campground. From here cross Rock Creek, then take the Sheltowee up to the Mark Branch Trail. The path crosses Mark Branch several times and also squeezes between boulders before reaching the Gobblers Arch Trail. Head back down the Gobblers Arch Trail. Your trip past Gobblers Arch and down to Rock Creek is super steep, but the loop is only four miles long.

Anglers will prefer sticking to Rock Creek. In its waters are trout and smallmouth bass. The river is stocked once a month from March until winter sets in. As summer moves along, the fish will move to the deeper holes. Park biologists suspect the trout are reproducing in this cool stream. I suspect you will have an enjoyable experience at Great Meadow.

To get there: From exit 11 on I-75 near Williamsburg, head west on KY 92 for 20 miles to US 27. Stay with Kentucky 92 for 6.5 more miles, crossing the Big South Fork on the Yamacraw Bridge. Just ahead, turn left on KY 1363, following it for 11.5 miles to the end of the blacktop. Turn right here on Forest Road 564, following FR 564 for 1.2 miles to Forest Road 137. Turn left on FR 137 and follow it for 4.5 miles to Great Meadows. The Deer Loop is first, on the right, and the Raccoon Loop is a bit farther, on the left.

KEY INFORMATION

Great Meadow
P.O. Box 429
Whitley City, KY 42653

Operated by: U.S. Forest Service

Information: (606) 376-5323, www.southernregion.fs.fed. us/boone

Open: Raccoon Loop open year-round; Deer Loop open April–November

Individual sites: 16

Each site has: Picnic table, fire ring, lantern post, tent pad

Site assignment: First come, first served; no reservation

Registration: No registration

Facilities: Water April–November only, vault toilets year-round

Parking: At campsites only

Fee: None

Elevation: 1,000 feet

Restrictions:

Pets—On 6-foot leash only

Fires—In fire rings only

Alcoholic beverages—At campsites only

Vehicles—None

Other—No trash cans; pack it in, pack it out

HOLLY BAY

London

As the baby boom generation ages I sometimes fear the pastime of tent camping will be lost in the graying of America. When the forest service revamps a campground, as they have at Holly Bay, it is heartening to see them install walk-in tent sites instead of turning everything into a more RV-compatible area. Holly Bay not only reassures me that tent camping is here to stay, but it also has some of the best tent campsites in this book. And these tent sites are set on one of Kentucky's cleanest, clearest lakes—Laurel River Lake—where recreation opportunities surround you.

Holly Bay actually has eight campsite loops, but you only need to be concerned about 3 of them. For the sake of completeness, the campground as a whole is neat, clean and well kept, making even the RV sites appealing. Drive past the campground entrance station, which is a nice safety measure, and turn right to reach the B Loop. An alluring foot trail leads from the tent camper parking area on the right to the walk-in campsites. Descend into thick woods on the hillside above Holly Bay. Site 1 is closest to the road. Sites 2 and 3 offer respites beneath a forest of pine, hemlock, oak, and other hardwoods. The other three tent sites in the B Loop are heavily shaded and offer obscured views of Holly Bay. The hillside sites have been leveled to make getting around the actual campsite easy.

CAMPGROUND RATINGS

Beauty:	★★★★★
Site privacy:	★★★★★
Site spaciousness:	★★★★
Quiet:	★★★★
Security:	★★★★★
Cleanliness/upkeep:	★★★★★

Holly Bay has first-rate walk-in tent sites on attractive Laurel River Lake.

CENTRAL

Just beyond the B Loop parking area is the C Loop parking area. The five walk-in sites offer a mixture of sun and shade. Site 3 is a double site. Site 4 is closest to the water and offers bay views. A comfort station with flush toilets is located by the B and C parking areas, as is a water spigot. If you stay in B or C loops, you must walk a bit to reach a bathhouse with a shower—they are located in between the two loops.

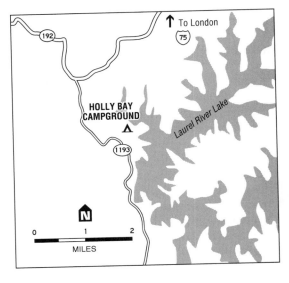

The other loop of note is G. Take the second right after the campground entrance station and park. G Loop has eight walk-in tent sites and some other sites with water and electricity. The bathhouse and shower lie across from the walk-in area. From the parking lot, take the foot trail into the woods and come to shady sites that offer maximum campsite privacy, even by the high walk-in tent standards set here. Three campsites are set on their own side trail toward the lake. Two of the remaining five sites are double sites. All these sites are very appealing and offer plenty of room for the most discriminating tent camper. Be advised that tent sites will fill on weekends during the heart of summer. The only reservable sites here at Holly Bay are D and H loops—not part of the walk-in tent area. I recommend coming early on Friday or during the week if possible; the setting at Laurel Lake is as appealing as the sites themselves. The campground hosts are here to answer your questions and also sell ice and wood to campers.

Being lakeside makes water recreation a natural. A boat launch offers easy access from the campground. If you didn't bring your own boat, one can be rented at Holly Bay Marina, just a short drive away. Anglers vie for bass, crappie, walleye, and even rainbow trout, which need cool, clear water to survive. On a hot summer day, you just might need cool waters of the popular swimming area by the Laurel River Lake Dam, just south of Holly Bay. The Army Corps of Engineers manages this swimming area. Also in their domain is a fishing pier for those without boats. If it's not hot enough, you can warm up by tracking the Sheltowee Trace Trail, which runs along the water's edge between Laurel River Lake and the campground, heading north and south for more miles than you can walk in a day. The Wintergreen Trail hooks into the Sheltowee Trace to make a one-mile loop for a leg stretcher hike. During the summer, naturalist programs are held at the campground amphitheater. Just remember, if you want to enjoy the best of the best in tent camping in Kentucky, come to Holly Bay, but come during the week if you can, or come early on Friday—just try to figure out a way to make it.

To get there: From exit 38 on I-75 near London, head west on KY 192 for 12.2 miles to KY 1193. Turn left on 1193 and follow it 3 miles to the campground, which will be on the left.

KEY INFORMATION

**Holly Bay
761 South Laurel Road
London, KY 40744**

Operated by: U.S. Forest Service

Information: (606) 864-4163; www.southernregion.fs.fed.us/boone/, reservations (877) 444-6777

Open: Mid-April—October

Individual sites: 19 walk-in tent sites, 75 other

Each site has: Picnic table, fire ring, upright grill, lantern post, tent pad; others have water and electricity

Site assignment: Tent sites are first come, first served; some others can be reserved

Registration: At campground entrance booth

Facilities: Hot showers, flush toilets, water spigots, pay phone, beverage machines

Parking: At walk-in parking areas and at campsites

Fee: $7 per night; others $15 and $19 per night

Elevation: 1,010 feet

Restrictions:

Pets—On 6-foot leash only

Fires—In fire rings only

Alcoholic beverages—At campsites only

Vehicles—Park in paved areas only

Other—14-day stay limit

PIKE RIDGE

Campbellsville

Green River Lake is green, just like the river it impounds. And it is backed by wooded green hills and tan rock bluffs. Pike Ridge Campground, one of the Army Corps of Engineers' newer campgrounds, lies at a point on the lake's edge, commanding a wide view of the surrounding land and water. The Corps impounded this lake in 1969 to control flooding on the Green River. Recreation is an added benefit of this flood-control effort. Come to Pike Ridge and you will appreciate the benefits of recreating along these scenic shores.

Pike Ridge Campground is actually on the Robinson Creek Arm of Green River Lake. Pass the campground entrance station and near the campground boat ramp. The main campground road is located here. These sites, numbers 1–19, now have water and electricity. Young trees, planted by the Corps, are just growing up and provide a little shade over the grassy area. They will provide more in time. Rocks have been placed on the shoreline to prevent erosion. All the sites overlook the water and are ideal for water lovers. Campsite spaciousness is average. At the end of the road is the swim beach, located on a small cove and makes for a safe swimming area for little campers. A small loop has eight campsites (sites 20–27) and is the least desirable. It has little shade and only two water access sites.

CAMPGROUND RATINGS

Beauty:	★★★
Site privacy:	★★
Site spaciousness:	★★★
Quiet:	★★★
Security:	★★★★★
Cleanliness/upkeep:	★★★★★

There is water everywhere at this campground on the shores of Green River Lake.

CENTRAL

The bigger loop, encompassing sites 28–53, is more appealing. Pass a comfort station and come to the campsites. The sites here are widespread and spacious. Begin a string of waterfront campsites (sites 31–40). These sites have limited shade, and boats can pull up directly to the campsite. The situation is the opposite at the back of the loop. Here, sites 44–53 are cut into thick woods and have superlative shade and high privacy, but they are not lakeside. I would take these sites during very hot weather, as the lake is just a short walk away. Turn away from the lake and pass five campsites (sites 56–60) near the entrance station. These are the least popular, though campers who come for peace and quiet enjoy them.

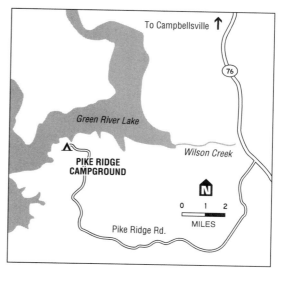

All sites are reservable, so no need to worry about getting shut out on summer holiday weekends. The above campsites numbers will help you make a blind reservation, but once here you will find a site to your liking for return adventures. A full-time campground attendant makes for a safer and more enjoyable trip. There is a small store just before entering the recreation area that offers firewood and limited supplies.

Most folks coming to Pike Ridge come for the lake access. A boat ramp makes getting on the water very easy. Many boaters like to fish, and Green River Lake is one of the premier muskellunge fisheries in Kentucky. This fish, commonly known as muskies, can grow in excess of three feet. More commonly sought and caught are smallmouth and largemouth bass, crappie, and bream. All campers can walk to the swim beach, though a few campsites are literally just a few feet away. The clear, green waters are an alluring reason to get wet. So is a hot Kentucky summer day. During cooler times, consider the nearby Pike Ridge Trail. Drive a half-mile back toward town away from the campground, and you will see a large parking area on the right. The trail begins beyond the gate; it extends for several miles along Pike Ridge, which divides the Robinson Creek and Green River arms of the lake. Mountain bikers will enjoy the trek as well. Return the way you came. Once you come to Pike Ridge, you will return here to camp, as well as hike, fish, swim, and boat.

To get there: From downtown Campbellsville, take KY 70 east for 4.2 miles to KY 76. Turn right on KY 76 and follow it 4.6 miles to Pike Ridge Road. Turn right on Pike Ridge Road and follow it for 5.5 miles to dead-end at the campground.

KEY INFORMATION

Pike Ridge
544 Lake Road
Campbellsville, KY 42718

Operated by: U.S. Army Corps of Engineers

Information: (270) 465-4463, www.lrl.usace.army.mil/grl, reservations (877) 444-6777

Open: Third Saturday in April–third Sunday in September

Individual sites: 60

Each site has: Picnic table, fire grate, lantern post; some have water and electricity

Site assignment: First come, first served, and by reservation

Registration: At campground entrance station

Facilities: Hot showers, water spigots, flush toilets

Parking: At campsites only

Fee: $12 per night standard sites, $17 per night electric sites

Elevation: 675 feet

Restrictions:

Pets—On 6-foot leash only

Fires—In fire rings only

Alcoholic beverages—At campsites only

Vehicles—Only 2 vehicles per site

Other—14-day stay limit

ROCKCASTLE

London

Upon reaching the Rockcastle area, I first came to the wide-open marina and boat launch area. The marina is small, but the openness of the setting took me back. Then I entered the green coolness of the mountainside campground. The hot summer day cooled a good ten degrees. Furthermore, the natural beauty around the campsites mightily impressed me. The sites are carved out of steep, heavily forested woodland punctuated by mammoth gray boulders.

Rockcastle Campground overlooks an impounded portion of the Rockcastle River just before it reaches the Cumberland River. Stone bluffs lie across the impoundment (Lake Cumberland). The dam of Lake Cumberland lies many miles downstream. Up here, the lake is but a long green ribbon of alluring water. Rockcastle Campground is stretched out on a long road that parallels the shoreline. Enter the shady tunnel of woods and immediately come to the first set of sites. Nearly all of them have to be reached by many steps leading down to leveled areas where the actual campsites lie. They all can be considered walk-in tent sites.

Beech, maple, hemlock, and oak trees reach high above the ground, while moss adorns huge boulders. Campsite 3 backs into a rock cliff. Away from the lake are a couple of vault toilets and a picnic pavilion for rainy days. The campground road

CAMPGROUND RATINGS

Beauty:	★★★★
Site privacy:	★★★★
Site spaciousness:	★★★
Quiet:	★★★
Security:	★★★
Cleanliness/upkeep:	★★★★

The campsites here are tucked into mountainside scenery overlooking the dammed portion of the Rockcastle River.

CENTRAL

continues to more well-separated and private sites. The
steep hillside does limit
campsite size. Some camp-
sites share a common walk-
way from the road, then
divide once they near the
lake. Some of the sites away
from the lake are very isolated. Pass the Dutch Branch
Trail, and then you'll reach
more appealing sites. These
sites are closer to the lake.
Water spigots are here, too.
Come to the auto turn-
around, which has six campsites. The first three, away
from the water, are little

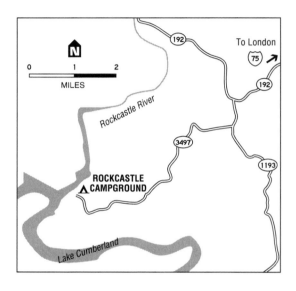

used. But sites 27, 28, and 29 are the campground's most popular. They abut
the lake and campers can pull their boats right up to the well-shaded camps.

Rockcastle will fill on holiday weekends, but campsites can be reserved.
However, you are asked to reserve for three nights if you do make a reservation. Your registration area, the marina, has a small camp store with supplies
and food for hungry campers that don't feel like cooking.

Hiking trails are a highlight here at Rockcastle; they leave directly from the
campground. Dutch Branch Trail makes a 0.7-mile loop in a rich forest, passing under several cliffs and rock shelters. A waterfall pours over the rocks
during rainy times. This trail also connects to the Scuttle Hole Overlook Trail.
This is a moderately easy path that passes three overlooks of Lake Cumberland and the Rockcastle River as it straddles a dramatic cliffline. The Ned
Branch Trail runs up a gorge beneath giant beech and buckeye trees, reaching
KY 3497, your campground access road, after two miles. Lakeside North Trail
spurs off the Ned Branch Trail and runs alongside the Rockcastle River for a
mile. Bank fishermen use this for a quiet angling experience. Lakeside South

Trail starts at the south end of the marina parking area and follows the shoreline of Lake Cumberland for four miles through Clarks Bottom. This trail is easy and has little elevation change. The Twin Branch Trail climbs away from Clark Bottom to reach the Ned Branch Trail, creating an eight-mile loop opportunity.

Walking around looking at all the water will make you want to get on the water yourself. Many campers will swim the lake near their campsites. Campers with their own boat can use the marina launch, or rent johnboats for angling or pontoon boats for pleasure riding and swimming. Motor up the Rockcastle River or up and down Lake Cumberland on the impounded Cumberland River, making for gorgeous valley boat trips. Don't miss this lake or your opportunity to tent camp at Rockcastle.

KEY INFORMATION

Rockcastle
761 South Laurel Road
London, KY 40744

Operated by: London Dock Marina

Information: (606) 864-5225, www.southernregion.fs.fed.us/boone

Open: Early May–September

Individual sites: 29

Each site has: Picnic table, fire ring, lantern post

Site assignment: First come, first served, and by reservation

Registration: At marina

Facilities: Water spigot, vault toilets

Parking: At campsites only

Fee: $10 per night

Elevation: 730 feet

Restrictions:

Pets—On 6-foot leash only

Fires—In fire rings only

Alcoholic beverages—At campsites only

Vehicles—None

Other—14-day stay limit

To get there: From exit 38 on I-75 near London, head west on KY 192 for 14 miles to KY 1193. Turn left on 1193 and follow it 1 mile to KY 3497. Turn right on 3497 and follow it 6 miles to dead-end at the campground.

EASTERN
KENTUCKY

ALUM FORD

Williamsburg

When inquiring with the park service about Alum Ford, the voice on the other line stated, "You might not like it. That place is primitive." She didn't know she was talking to a tent camper who likes their campgrounds that way! Upon my arrival in person, Alum Fork did not disappoint—it is primitive indeed. Located near a boat landing on the Big South Fork, the campground is strung along a dead-end gravel road on the edge of the river gorge. What makes it even better is all the recreational opportunities nearby—like hiking, boating, fishing, and swimming.

But first the campground. Be watchful along the road to Alum Ford landing, for the road to the campground spurs unexpectedly to the left, just before reaching the Big South Fork of the Cumberland River. The road is cut into the side of the hill. After passing a wet-weather stream, you begin to wonder where the campground is going to be in this forest of smooth beech trees, shaggy hickories, and upright oaks. Crane your neck and look left, up the steep hill to campsite 1. Steps have been cut into the hillside here, leading to a platform where campers look out on the forest. Campsite 2 is on the right-hand side of the road, closer to the river. It is downslope of the gravel road, as is campsite 3. The next one, site 4, is up the hill on the left.

Pass the water spigot, which is turned off, and the vault toilets. Just past this is

CAMPGROUND RATINGS

Beauty:	★★★★
Site privacy:	★★★★
Site spaciousness:	★★★★
Quiet:	★★★★
Security:	★★★
Cleanliness/upkeep:	★★★

Camp on the Big South Fork near Kentucky's highest waterfall.

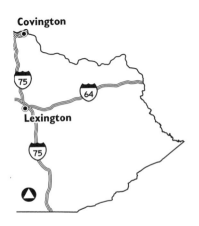

EASTERN

campsite 5, also cut into the hillside above the road, which ends just ahead near campsite 6. Here, the bluff is so steep that the park service has erected a fence to keep careless campers from taking an unintentional tumble to the river. Campers who stay at site 7 have to park here and walk a bit to reach their site, which is the most secluded in the campground. But how much seclusion do you need at a place with only seven campsites? Alum Ford rarely fills, save for holiday weekends.

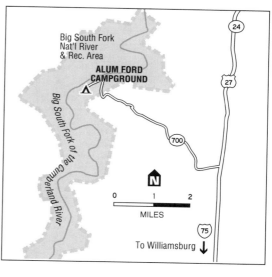

All the sites are wooded, but there are obscured views of the river below and a tall rock bluff on the far side of the gorge. Shade will be welcome during the hot summer months. But if you get too hot, the river is just a five-minute walk down a footpath, so don't take the quick route over the bluff. Swimmers can enjoy the landing at Alum Ford. The upper reaches of Lake Cumberland extend to Alum Ford, making for a slack or minimal current most of the time. Bring your canoe or small boat. Paddling enthusiasts can explore the waters here, fishing for smallmouth bass and sunfish. If you want more exciting water, head upstream and run the gorge, starting at Worley or Yamacraw, then ease your way down to Alum Ford.

Hikers have a special treat here. The master path of Kentucky, the 269-mile Sheltowee Trace, passes right through the campground on the gravel road. It is marked by the turtle blaze on the trees. Head north on the Sheltowee for 1.3 miles along the river to reach the Yahoo Falls Scenic Area. Here a group of trails takes you all through this special slice of the Big South Fork. Walk to a short distance to Yahoo Falls, Kentucky's highest at 113 feet. A veil of water spills over a lip of rock into a pool that lies in the amphitheater of an immense rock house, where Indians once resided over 9,000 years ago. Ambitious hikers will continue on to Yahoo Arch, over a ridge, then drop down Negro Creek, which leads to the Big South Fork. Cruise along the river and return to Alum Ford. Nearby Princess Falls is south on the Sheltowee Trace from the junction with Negro Creek. The beauty and recreation opportunities of this area are obviously much larger than the intimate Alum Ford campground.

To get there: From exit 11 on I-75 near Williamsburg, head west on KY 92 for 20 miles to US 27. Turn right on 27 and follow it for 6.5 miles north to KY 700. Turn left on 700 and follow it 5.5 miles the Alum Ford fee station. Veer left onto the gravel campground road just before reaching the landing.

Alum Ford
Route 3, Box 401
Oneida, TN 37841

Operated by: National Park Service

Information: (931) 879-3625, www.nps.gov/biso

Open: Year-round

Individual sites: 7

Each site has: Picnic table, fire ring, lantern post, tent pad, some have upright grills

Site assignment: First come, first served; no reservation

Registration: Self-registration on site

Facilities: Vault toilets (bring your own water)

Parking: At campsites only

Fee: $5 per night

Elevation: 800 feet

Restrictions

  Pets—On 6-foot leash only

  Fires—In fire rings only

  Alcoholic beverages—At campsites only

  Vehicles—Maximum 2 vehicles per site

  Other—14-day stay limit

CARTER CAVES STATE PARK

Olive Hill

If you like a wide variety of activities con-centrated into one area, Carter Caves is the place for you. The fact that it is honey-combed with numerous caverns is given away in its name. Visitors can tour them in varied fashion from easy walking tours to down and dirty cave crawls. But there's more—as in 20 miles of hiking trails, canoe trips on lakes and rivers, fishing, boating, and horseback riding. With all this to do, you probably won't be spending much time in the campground, which is a mixture of desirable and less-than-desirable sites.

Luckily for tent campers, the camp-ground is divided into two distinct sec-tions. The main campground will affirm your decision to be a tent camper. A full 89 sites are laid out in subdivision-like fash-ion, many too close together, though there are a few good shaded sites. Tent campers should ignore this area and instead head for the tall pines of the primitive area, where 30 campsites are laid out in a teardrop-shaped loop. The sites under the pines have a lush grassy understory that is appealing but does little for campsite pri-vacy. The sites on the outside of the loop are more spacious and slope down the side of the ridge. Toward the back of the loop are the less-delineated but larger sites. Two bathhouses and several water spigots serve the campground. A small camp store has limited supplies.

CAMPGROUND RATINGS

Beauty:	★★★
Site privacy:	★★★
Site spaciousness:	★★★★
Quiet:	★★★
Security:	★★★★
Cleanliness/upkeep:	★★★★

The exceptional list of activities makes this campground more appealing than it might otherwise be.

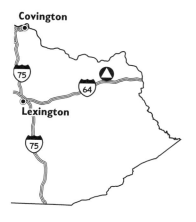

EASTERN

Carter Caves Campground is open year-round. Only on nice weekends during high summer does the campground fill. Visiting here during the cold season offers a unique attraction, as the temperature in the caves stays the same year-round. This can also be an advantage during a hot or rainy summer day. Three primary tours are available for campers. The Cascade Cave Tour, about a mile in length, is highlighted by a visit to an underground waterfall that is inside the cave. The X

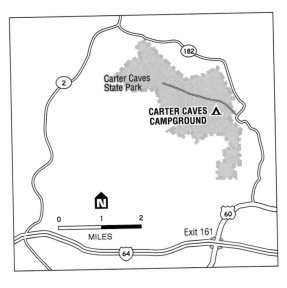

Cave, named after the shape of its passages, is 0.25-mile long and contains the park's largest and oldest cave formation. Saltpetre Cave is the most historic. Saltpeter was extracted from the cave and used to make gunpowder during the War of 1812. It is also the coldest cave in the park. On weekends, cave tours take off about six times a day. Get your tickets at the Welcome Center. Rangers also lead rough, strenuous crawling tours that pass through tight, wet places. Bring a flashlight, clothes you can get wet in, and kneepads for these tours. One other cave you can visit, the Bat Cave, is open only during the summer, In winter, thousands of bats make this their home. This is also a rugged tour.

Park programs are not limited to the caves. The park prides itself on many guided tours above ground. Take a horseback ride from the riding stable. Rangers lead canoe trips on Smoky Valley Lake, providing the boats and interesting information about the park. Rental fishing and pedal boats are also available on the 40-acre impoundment that has angling for largemouth bass, crappie, and bluegill. Rangers also lead canoe trips down Tygart's Creek. Other programs include group singing, ice cream socials, folk tales, and nature walks.

While here, you can also entertain yourself on some 20 miles of trails that course through the rugged land. Shorter paths lead to natural bridges, arches, and rock formations. The longer Carter Caves Cross-Country Trail makes a 7.2-mile loop. Even longer is a 10-mile loop through Tygarts Forest on the Kiser Hollow Multi-Use Trail.

More citified pastimes include lounging by the swimming pool, a nine-hole golf course, and mini-golf. You might need a little bit of this more conventional relaxation after touring the natural features of Carter Caves.

KEY INFORMATION

Carter Caves State Park
344 Caveland Drive
Olive Hill, KY 41164

Operated by: Kentucky State Parks

Information: (606) 286-4411, www.kystateparks.com

Open: Year-round

Individual sites: 30 primitive sites, 89 water and electric sites

Each site has: Picnic table, fire ring; others have water and electricity

Site assignment: First come, first served; no reservation

Registration: At campground check station

Facilities: Hot showers, flush toilets, laundry, camp store

Parking: At campsites only

Fee: $8.50 per night primitive sites, $16 per night other

Elevation: 900 feet

Restrictions:

Pets—On 6-foot leash only

Fires—In fire rings only

Alcoholic beverages—Not allowed

Vehicles—None

Other—14-day stay limit

To get there: From exit 161 on I-64 west of Grayson, take US 60 east for 1.4 miles to KY 182. Turn left on KY 182 and continue for 3 miles to a left turn into the park.

CLEAR CREEK

Owingsville

My first impression of Clear Creek Campground was the sight of Clear Creek Lake and its translucent waters backed by green, wooded ridges. After that, things only got better. A front had moved through, clearing the haze from the summer sky. Sunbeams shot from above and filtered through the trees. The temperature was just perfect. I rolled into the campground, picked a site, then ran over and looked at Clear Creek. Then came the dilemma—what to do first on such a day? Should I walk some of the 30 miles of trails of the nearby Pioneer Weapons Wildlife Management Area, fish Clear Creek Lake, check out the old iron furnace, drive the Zilpo Scenic Byway, or see the arch south of here on the Sheltowee Trace?

I set up camp first. The campground is laid out in a flat along Clear Creek. Enter the campground, where the road splits along the flat. Take the left road up the flat to sites 1–12. A lush forest of oaks, dogwoods, and tulip trees shades the camps, which are well separated by these trees and thick undergrowth. It is hard to see one site from another. Several campsites lie streamside and get snapped up first. Reach a mini-loop at road's end with sites spoking out from it. A modern vault toilet and water pump lie in the middle of the loop. Campsites 13–21 lie to the right of the road split. A campground host occupies the first site and keeps the campground in good

CAMPGROUND RATINGS

Beauty: ★★★★★
Site privacy: ★★★★★
Site spaciousness: ★★★★
Quiet: ★★★
Security: ★★★★
Cleanliness/upkeep: ★★★★

Clear Creek lies next to the best mountain biking and hiking in the northern Daniel Boone National Forest.

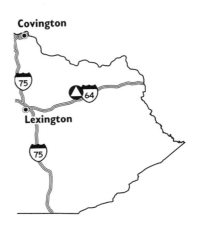

EASTERN

shape. There are plenty of large, well-separated sites. A few hemlocks add even more shade to the sites. A mini-loop with quality campsites lies at the end of this road as well.

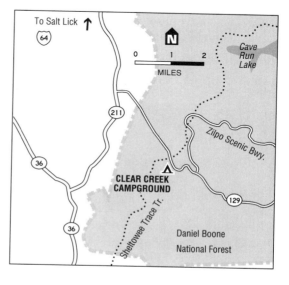

The nearby Zilpo Scenic Byway is a mixed blessing. It is great for auto touring and exploring other areas of the forest, but noise from it is audible from the camp-ground. Fortunately, this is not a heavily used commer-cial road—far from it. Clear Creek will fill on many pret-ty weekends, mainly due to overflow from the much larger and busier Zilpo Campground, which is down the scenic byway.

After setting up camp, I cruised over to the Pioneer Weapons Wildlife Man-agement Area adjacent to the campground. Several mountain bikers who were camped at Clear Creek mentioned there is good mountain biking here. Unfortunately, I left my bike at home, so I settled for exploring Buck Creek Trail by foot, after taking the Sheltowee Trace north a bit. On the way, I saw a doe and fawn feeding at the edge of the clear stream. Later, I cruised down to check out the Clear Creek Iron furnace, where, in the mid-1800s ore was melt-ed into "pigs" for shipment down the Ohio River. These pigs were then con-verted to wheels for the locomotives of the day. I continued down the Clear Creek Lake Trail to Clear Creek Lake. Unfortunately, I left my canoe at home too. This body of water is a "no gas motors" lake, making for a quiet canoeing experience where you can also fish.

The next day, I decided to walk south, down the Sheltowee Trace. After a couple of miles I reached an arch on the right of the trail. The arch itself held appeal, but a view from the top of it added to the hike. Unfortunately, I left my camera at home as well. Later still, I took a scenic drive. Fortunately, I did have my car with me. I motored the Zilpo Scenic Byway and stopped at Tater Knob Fire Tower. Built in 1934, the structure was restored in 1993 and is now on the National Historic Lookout Tower Register. Cave Run Lake and the hills and valleys of the forest stretched out on the horizon. I reflected that on my next Clear Creek adventure I'd bring my bike, canoe, fishing rod, and camera.

To get there: From exit 123 on I-64 near Owingsville, take US 60 East for 6.5 miles to Salt Lick. Turn right onto KY 211. (Ignore the left turn on 211 that precedes the right turn.) Follow KY 211 for 3 miles to KY 129. Take a left on 129, Clear Creek Road, and follow it 3 miles to the campground, on your right.

KEY INFORMATION

Clear Creek
2375 KY 801 South
Morehead, KY 40351

Operated by: U.S. Forest Service

Information: (606) 784-6428, www.southernregion.fs.fed.us/boone

Open: Early April–October

Individual sites: 21

Each site has: Picnic table, fire ring, lantern post, tent pad

Site assignment: First come, first served; no reservation

Registration: Self-registration on site

Facilities: Water spigots, vault toilets

Parking: At campsites only

Fee: $8 per night

Elevation: 770 feet

Restrictions:

Pets—On 6-foot leash only

Fires—In fire rings only

Alcoholic beverages—At campsites only

Vehicles—Maximum 2 vehicles per site

Other—14-day stay limit

CUMBERLAND GAP NATIONAL HISTORICAL PARK

Middlesboro

This national park, situated where Kentucky, Tennessee, and Virginia meet, is one of the South's hidden jewels. I have been coming here for many years and continue to learn and enjoy more about this historical preserve with each visit. It is centered on Cumberland Gap, which is a break in the Appalachian Mountains used by animals, Indians, settlers, and armies for entrance into Kentucky from points east. Today, you can pitch your tent in a fine campground and explore the park's history on its extensive trail system.

The campground is situated on a heavily wooded sloping ridgeline. Its 160 sites sprawl widely in this woodland. Imagine a huge loop with roads cutting across the loop. Sites are situated on the outside of the grand loop and on both sides of the inner roads. Loops B and C have electric hookups and are the domain of the big rigs. Other than that, the many sites offer every possibility of sun and shade combinations. Overall, the sites are average in size. The thick woodland of pine, dogwood, oak, maple, and hickory delivers superb privacy. And with such a large underused campground, you can almost always find a site with no one around. Three full-service bathhouses with adjacent water spigots serve the campground. In the cooler months there may only be another straggler or two to share the whole camping area. I recommend visiting

CAMPGROUND RATINGS

Beauty:	★★★★
Site privacy:	★★★★★
Site spaciousness:	★★★
Quiet:	★★★
Security:	★★★★
Cleanliness/upkeep:	★★★★★

Explore Cumberland Gap's rich human history via 50 miles of hiking trails.

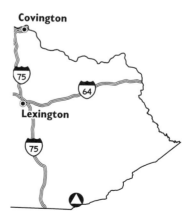

EASTERN

the park during spring and fall, as summer can be hot and there is no water recreation. But summer is better than not at all. The campground never fills, so this is one place you can always count on a campsite.

Daniel Boone is the most famous of the Cumberland Gap travelers, but Dr. Thomas Walker was actually the first European to cross the gap, in 1750. By the 1770s, settlers began pouring over the gap into Kentucky, leading to its statehood in 1792. Cumberland Gap decreased in importance as other western travel routes opened, though during the Civil War it saw a resurgence of activity as both sides occupied the gap's heights. Today, visitors can see an iron furnace, remnants of two Civil War forts, and a reconstructed pioneer settlement. Natural features include Skylight Cave, Cudjo Cave, and far-reaching views from the Pinnacle, and my personal favorite, White Rocks.

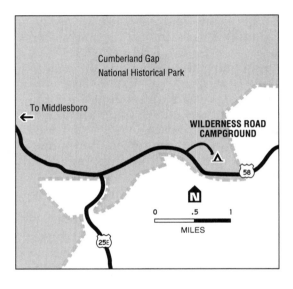

Those wanting to hike can reach a system of trails of varying lengths that spur directly from the Wilderness Road Campground. Grab a detailed trail map at the campground entrance station to see the available options. Shorter paths include the Greenleaf Nature Trail, the Colson Trail, and the Honey Tree Spur Trail. Longer trails include the Lewis Hollow Trail, which leads to Skylight Cave and the Pinnacle, and the Gibson Gap Trail. You can make a 10-mile loop out of the campground using the Gibson Gap, Ridge Trail, and Lewis Hollow Trail. Or drive over to the Cudjo Cave Area and take the Wilderness Road Trail to the Tri-State Trail and Tri-State Peak, where you can stand in Tennessee, Kentucky, and Virginia at once. From here, the Cumberland Trail heads south to ultimately reach Signal Mountain near Chattanooga.

My favorite hike is in the east end of the park. Take US 58 east to Ewing, then turn left on VA 724. Take the Ewing Trail up to White Rocks, with its fantastic view south into the ridge and valley country of Virginia and Tennessee. Make the side trip to Sand Cave, which is a huge overhang with a sandy floor, then loop back down to the trailhead. Take a ranger-guided walk back in time to the Hensley Settlement, a collection of pioneer homes that rivals anything in Southern Appalachians. It is absolutely worth a visit. Tour reservations are recommended. Take time to stop by the park visitor center with its many interesting displays about Cumberland Gap. Other ranger-guided activities are held daily during summer. No matter if it is spring, summer, or fall, make time to visit this treasure shared by three states.

> **To get there:** From the junction of US 25E and KY 74 in Middlesboro, head south on 25E for 2 miles to US 58. Turn left on US 58 and follow it east 2 miles to the Wilderness Road Campground entrance road on your left.

KEY INFORMATION

Cumberland Gap National Historical Park
Box 1848
Middlesboro, KY 40965

Operated by: National Park Service

Information: (606) 248-2817, www.nps.gov/cuga

Open: Year-round

Individual sites: 121 primitive; 49 electric

Each site has: Picnic table, fire ring

Site assignment: First come, first served; no reservation

Registration: Self-registration on site

Facilities: Hot showers, flush toilets, water spigots

Parking: At campsites only

Fee: $10 per night primitive sites; $15 per night electric sites

Elevation: 1,300 feet

Restrictions:

Pets—On 6-foot leash only

Fires—In fire rings only

Alcoholic beverages—At campsites only

Vehicles—None

Other—14-day stay limit

KINGDOM COME STATE PARK

Cumberland

If someone where to threaten to blow you to kingdom come, you might not mind if this state park were your destination. Kingdom Come State Park, the state's highest park, is truly a land of superlatives and deserves more visitors than it gets. I rate it as one of Kentucky's finest state parks. The natural setting is ideal—the heavily wooded ridgetop of Pine Mountain is speckled with numerous rock outcrops, each offering scenic vistas of the surrounding Appalachian Mountains, including Kentucky's highest point (Black Mountain at over 4,000 feet). July visitors might also catch the rhododendron blooming. This is also bear country, so don't be too surprised if you run into a bruin on the trails here. The campground is small but excellent and makes for a fine base camp to explore the trails and roads that run through the surrounding high country.

Before you head toward the campground, stop by the stone gazebo at the park entrance and grab a quick view. This vista looks east, across the Poor Fork Cumberland River Valley and to the even higher mountains of eastern Harlan County. Down below is the town of Cumberland. The sight might inspire you to head to Log Rock, but wait until after you are situated. Continue up the mountain a little more and take a left turn into the camping area. Immediately dip down to reach four well-groomed, well-kept campsites at the head

CAMPGROUND RATINGS

Beauty:	★★★★
Site privacy:	★★★
Site spaciousness:	★★★
Quiet:	★★★★★
Security:	★★★★
Cleanliness/upkeep:	★★★★★

This is Kentucky's highest campground.

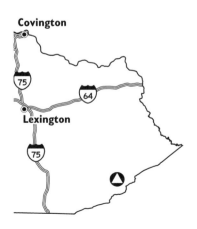

EASTERN

of a small hollow. The hollow isn't even, but the campsites have been leveled for better eating and sleeping. Overhead is a forest of maple, pine, and oak. Bathrooms are just a few steps down the hollow. The water spigot is a few steps farther down, toward a picnic shelter that would make a good respite in a rainstorm. A horseshoe pit lies across from the campground.

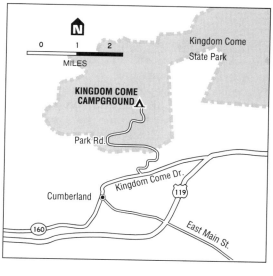

Some might think twice about driving a long way to this first come, first served campground. Don't worry. The park staff assured me that no campers are ever turned away. They encourage visitors and will simply put you at a site on the adjacent picnic area. The picnic sites resemble the campsites, except they lack a tent pad and lantern post. The bathroom and water spigot are just as close. Remember, keep all your food stored in the trunk of your car overnight or if you leave the campsite for a while. This is not to scare you off—remember that bears want your food, not your flank. And it helps the bears, for a wild bear that eats wild food stays wild. On the other hand, as the saying goes, "A fed bear is a dead bear." Human food–habituated bears become brazen in their quest for food, and ultimately end up being relocated, shot, or poached.

So now that you have put your food away, take a hike. This park is ideal for hiking, with several interconnected trails that cover the highlights of Kingdom Come. The Log Rock Trail is just across the road from the camping area. Take it for another view to the east. It ends up at the stone gazebo and the park lake, where trout, bass, and catfish can be caught. Pedal boats are also available for rent. The Laurel Trail leads from the lake to the cave amphitheater that is actually a giant rockhouse where bleachers are situated for events taking place in a totally natural setting. Keep up the Powerline Trail to access Raven Rock, which is at the top of the rockhouse and offers more views. Here, the rock faces angles down the side of Pine Mountain.

There are several other trails roaming the park. While hiking the Raven Rock Trail, I enjoyed some blueberries, and on the way down on the Groundhog Trail, I came upon some fresh bear scat. The bear had been eating blueberries too. The Little Shepherd Trail is open to hikers, bikers, and cars. It leads 13 miles east to US 119, and another 25 miles to Whitesburg. Allow plenty of time on this road if you drive it. And allow yourself some time to visit this fine state park. Supplies can be had down in the town of Cumberland. Also down there is the Kentucky Coal Mining Museum and the School House Inn Historic Site.

To get there: From the junction of US 421 and US 119 near Harlan, head north on US 119 for 22 miles to Kingdom Come Drive. Turn left on Kingdom Come Drive and follow it 0.7 mile to Park Road. Turn right on Park Road and follow it 1.3 miles to the state park.

KEY INFORMATION

Kingdom Come State Park
Box M
Cumberland, KY 40823

Operated by: Kentucky State Parks

Information: (606) 589-2479, www.kystateparks.com

Open: Year-round

Individual sites: 4

Each site has: Picnic table, fire ring, lantern post, tent pad

Site assignment: First come, first served; no reservation

Registration: At Visitor Center or ranger will come by and register you

Facilities: Flush toilets, water spigot

Parking: At campsites only

Fee: $5 per night

Elevation: 2,350 feet

Restrictions

Pets—On 6-foot leash only

Fires—In fire rings only

Alcoholic beverages—Not allowed

Vehicles—None

Other—14-day stay limit

K O O M E R   R I D G E

Slade

The Red River Gorge Geological Area has, among other things, more natural arches within it than anywhere else in the East. The work of 70 million years of wind and water has resulted in over 100 arches and uncountable rock formations of other kinds. Sixty miles of foot trails can access many of these arches, as can short walks from scenic roads that penetrate the geological area. And to top it off, Koomer Ridge is an ideal tent campground. But there is one little negative—you can hear the autos driving the nearby Bert Combs Mountain Parkway from the campground. I am no fan of car noise, but I found the positives of Koomer Ridge overwhelm the one negative. Now to the good parts.

As you pass the campground host, veer right into this ridgetop camp. Pass well-separated, shady sites nestled off the road, and swing right on a small loop. The sites are on the inside of the loop, which often spells crummy camps, but not here at Koomer. These sites are in good shape and offer more than adequate privacy and spaciousness. At the end of the loop is a fully equipped bathhouse in mint condition (and kept that way by campground hosts). The main campground road continues along with widespread sites situated beneath pines, oaks, maples, and occasional hemlocks. Many of the sites are walk-ins on the ridgeline, while others are classic pull-in sites. The road ends in a small loop

CAMPGROUND RATINGS

Beauty:	★★★★★
Site privacy:	★★★★
Site spaciousness:	★★★★
Quiet:	★★★
Security:	★★★★
Cleanliness/upkeep:	★★★★★

Koomer Ridge provides access to the Red River Gorge Geological Area.

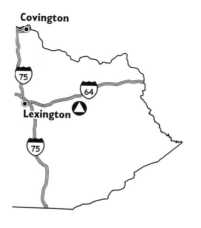

EASTERN

with good sites spoking into the woods. I stayed at campsite 39.

Eleven more sites (numbers 44–54) are off by themselves. The first two lie along a separate road that leads to a walk-in tent camper parking area. Three sites spur off the Hidden Arch Trail—these are less shady than the campsites on the main loop. The remaining six sites are connected to the parking area by gravel paths. Tent campers would proudly pitch their tent at any of these sites, all served by a water spigot and vault toilet (though water is shut off during winter). Water spigots and newer-style vault toilets are spread throughout the rest of the campground. Koomer Ridge will fill on most weekends. If you want to get a site, try to make it here by noon on Friday. During the week you will have no problems.

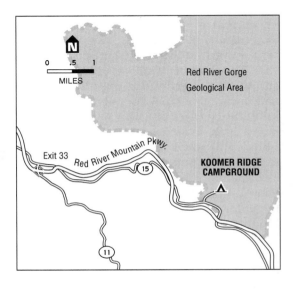

Hikers can explore the geological area directly from the campground. Start with the Cliff Trail that offers views from rock bluffs. The Silvermine Arch Trail descends to a wide arch backed by a tall bluff. The Hidden Arch Trail swings around a bluffline to a smaller arch, then connects to the Koomer Ridge Trail, which is your ticket to the heart of the geological area. Longer loop possibilities can be made from Koomer Ridge Trail, which connects other trails.

If you don't want to walk a trail, take a scenic drive. On your way here you passed the Tunnel Ridge Road, which leads through an old railroad tunnel. Beyond here is Star Gap Arch and other features like Double Arch, all accessible by a short path. Chimney Top Rock Road leads to Chimney Top Rock and Princess Arch. It also overlooks the National Wild and Scenic Red River, a destination in its own right. Kentucky 715 takes drivers to Skybridge, a huge arch with a far-reaching view of the Clifty Wilderness, which lies east of the geological area. KY 715 continues along the Red River and passes Gladie Cabin, a log house from the 1800s. The visitor center here is open during the warm season. Other trails spur from these roads. Grab a map at the campground entrance and take off; just don't let a little auto noise bother you.

To get there: From exit 33 on Bert Combs Mountain Parkway near Slade, take KY 15 South (it actually runs east) for 5 miles to the campground on your left.

KEY INFORMATION

Koomer Ridge
705 West College Avenue
Stanton, KY 40380

Operated by: U.S. Forest Service

Information: (606) 663-2852, www.southernregion.fs.fed.us/boone

Open: Whole campground, mid-April–October; sites 44–54, year-round

Individual sites: 54

Each site has: Picnic table, fire ring, lantern post, tent pad

Site assignment: First come, first served; no reservation

Registration: Self-registration on site

Facilities: Hot showers, flush toilets, pay phone; vault toilets and no water during winter

Parking: At campsites and at walk-in tent parking area

Fee: $10 per night mid-April–October; $5 per night rest of year

Elevation: 1,240 feet

Restrictions:
  Pets—On 6-foot leash only
  Fires—In fire rings only
  Alcoholic beverages—At campsites only
  Vehicles—Maximum 2 vehicles per site
  Other—14-day stay limit

NATURAL BRIDGE STATE PARK

Slade

You should definitely visit Natural Bridge State Park, but not if you come just for the camping. The campground is average, but the superlative beauty of this state park overrides the qualities of the campground. The park's centerpiece, Natural Bridge, is just the start of many sights to see. Other activities include hiking, swimming, and nature study. Come here to check out the unusual rock formations, ride the skylift, or fish. Luckily for tent campers, each of the two camping areas have primitive sites designed for them. And that certainly makes the campground much more bearable.

The first campground, Middle Fork, lies along the banks of the Middle Fork of the Red River. Pass the entrance station and enter a packed, open area with too few trees, too much pavement, and too many RVs. The sites in this loop have water and electricity. A road spurs off the loop and leads over a hill away from RV central. A sign by the road states "Tents Only." The road drops down and runs along the banks of Middle Fork into a different camping world. These are the preferred sites at Middle Fork Campground. The 11 sites are large and mostly shaded, but an understory of grass reduces privacy. The gurgling river is your front yard and a wooded hill backs the streamside camping flat. The bathhouse is back at the RV area. One site lies at the end of the auto turn-

CAMPGROUND RATINGS

Beauty: ★★★
Site privacy: ★★★
Site spaciousness: ★★★
Quiet: ★★★
Security: ★★★★
Cleanliness/upkeep: ★★★★★

The Natural Bridge is only the beginning of many natural and man-made attractions here.

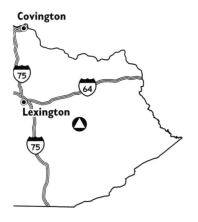

Covington

75

64

Lexington

75

EASTERN

around. Tent campers will enjoy these sites most.

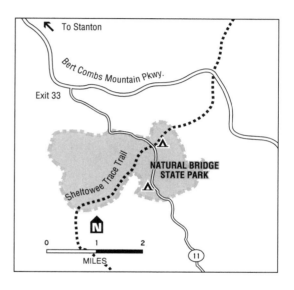

The Whittleton Camping Area is a mile distant. It is also a mix of terrible RV sites and tolerable tent sites. Pass the entrance booth and turn right on a little bridge over Whittleton Creek. The 20 tent campsites here loop around a bathhouse that is as close as the Middle Fork Campground bathhouse is distant. The tent sites here are in a mix of sun and shade. They are a little on the small side. Some of the best sites are directly along Whittleton Creek. Privacy and spaciousness are limited. A dead-end road continues up Whittleton Creek and has several pull-in campsites with water and electricity that are decent if you prefer a larger site. Neither campground fills often, save for summer holidays. In the unlikely event that you can't get a site, just stay at the Hemlock Lodge, where good meals are served.

The natural attributes of the land, namely Natural Arch, are the reasons this park is here in the first place. Natural Arch can be reached on one of the many miles of trails that course through the park. The Original Trail reaches the arch after 0.7 mile and connects to other paths passing such features as Balanced Rock, Battleship Rock, Devils Gulch, Needles Eye, and Lookout Point. Pick up a good map at the campground entrance booth. If you don't feel like walking, take the skylift to within 200 yards of Natural Arch. Of course, you will have to walk those last 200 yards. On the opposite end of the spectrum is the Sand Gap Trail, which makes a 7.5-mile loop around the park.

The Daniel Boone National Forest surrounds this state park. Whittleton Campground is on the edge of the national forest. From here, the Whittleton

Trail follows an old railroad grade to Whittleton Arch a mile distant at the base of a sandstone cliff. If none of these trails are long enough, the Sheltowee Trace makes part of its trek from Tennessee to northern Kentucky directly through the park.

An activities and nature center focuses on the natural aspect of the park and offers daily programs for kid and adults alike. Folks can head to Hoedown Island Lake to paddle around in small boats or see the weekly square dancing held on the lake's island. Families can play mini-golf, swim in a big pool, or fish Middle Fork and Mill Creek Lake. So accept the fact that though the campgrounds aren't the world's greatest, they will do—especially considering the surroundings.

KEY INFORMATION

**Natural Bridge State Park
2135 Natural Bridge Road
Slade, KY 40376**

Operated by: Kentucky State Parks

Information: (606) 663-2214, www.kystateparks.com

Open: Mid-April–October

Individual sites: 31 primitive sites, 55 water and electric sites

Each site has: Primitive sites have picnic table, fire ring, lantern post; others have water and electricity

Site assignment: First come, first served; no reservation

Registration: At campground entrance booth

Facilities: Hot showers, flush toilets, pay phone, laundry

Parking: At campsites only

Fee: $8.50 per night primitive sites, $16 per night water and electric sites

Elevation: 850 feet

Restrictions:

Pets—On 6-foot leash only

Fires—In fire rings only

Alcoholic beverages—At camp-sites only

Vehicles—Maximum 2 vehicles per site

Other—Maximum 8 campers per site

To get there: From exit 33 on the Bert Combs Mountain Parkway near Slade, head south on KY 11 for 3 miles to the state park.

PINE MOUNTAIN STATE PARK

Pineville

This state park has a campground whose attendance has inexplicably fallen over the past few years. Sure, it is an older campground and the sites are on the small side, but Pine Mountain makes a great summer and fall destination. At 2,000 feet, the campground is cool in the summer and in fall puts on quite a leaf display. Don't make the mistake others have and miss this place. Chained Rock, the park's signature feature, is an Appalachian landmark. In the 1920s, some whimsical hikers attached a chain from a seemingly precarious boulder to a more substantial rock face. Far-reaching views, arches, waterfalls, and rich forests await forest travelers on other trails.

As I pulled up to the campground, a sign stated "Attention Campers, No Electric Hookups." That sure got my attention. I knew this was a destination for tent campers only. Pass the campground entrance station and enter the hilltop camp. A big loop with paved campsite pull-ins winds around a rolling ridgetop forest of pine and oak that shades the campground. You will notice the sites are overly close together and somewhat small. Normally, this would be a problem, but the campground stays more empty than full, so you can usually get a site with no one on either side of you. The uneven terrain makes pitching a tent a problem at some of the sites. Again, there should be

CAMPGROUND RATINGS

Beauty:	★★★
Site privacy:	★★★
Site spaciousness:	★★
Quiet:	★★★★★
Security:	★★★★★
Cleanliness/upkeep:	★★★★★

Chained Rock is a Southern Appalachian icon.

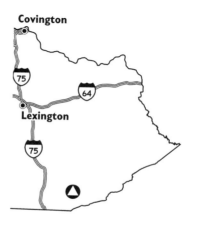

Covington

75

64

Lexington

75

EASTERN

enough open sites to find a more level tent area. Pass an old-time picnic shelter with a fireplace that makes for a welcome respite from rain; it has picnic tables beneath it. The bathhouse is just past the picnic shelter and looks pretty old-timey too.

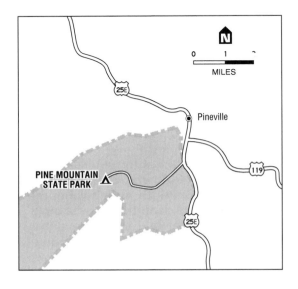

The loop splits, and to the left, a road runs along the ridgeline. The best campsites are on this road. What they lack in size, they make up in privacy. These sites are well separated from one another. Return to the original loop and come to more campsites that are a little pinched in and pretty uneven. An occasional site is fine. Don't be discouraged. Many quality sites are here; just be picky.

After you have carefully chosen a site, visit the natural features of the park. Here, you can't go wrong. A must-see is Chained Rock.; you passed the side road to it on the way in. Take the half-mile path and see the rock and the vista from here into Pineville and the mountains beyond. The Laurel Cove Trail spurs off here and passes a natural bridge before it dips down the mountain. The Rock Hotel Trail also leaves from the Chained Rock trailhead and heads one mile to this rock formation. Another series of trails leaves from the park lodge area. By the way, they also serve a decent meal at the lodge and offer good views from the dining room. Check out the Log Stairway, Fern Garden, and the Lost Trail. The Hemlock Garden Trail leads to Inspiration Point. The Nature Center is also near the Lodge. Pine Mountain has a full-time naturalist and presents nature programs. A modern swimming pool is open during high summer, as is a mini-golf course. There is also a new regulation-size golf course. A special event in the park is the Mountain Laurel Festival; this is held in May when the mountain laurel blooms. If you can't make the festival, try to get here during this time to see the pink and white blooms of the plant so abundant on Pine Mountain. Tent campers are one thing you won't find in abundance here. Even after visiting the park, I still don't understand why.

KEY INFORMATION

Pine Mountain State Park
1050 State Park Road
Pineville, KY 40977

Operated by: Kentucky State Park

Information: (606) 337-3066, www.kystateparks.com

Open: Year-round

Individual sites: 32

Each site has: Picnic table, fire ring, upright grill

Site assignment: First come, first served; no reservation

Registration: At campground entrance station

Facilities: Hot showers, flush toilets, water spigots

Parking: At campsites only

Fee: $8.50 per night

Elevation: 2,000 feet

Restrictions:

Pets—On 6-foot leash only

Fires—In fire rings only

Alcoholic beverages—Not allowed

Vehicles—Maximum 2 vehicles per site

Other—14-day stay limit

To get there: From the junction of US 25E and US 119 in Pineville, head south 0.5 mile to the park entrance on your right. Follow the park road 7 miles to the campground, on your left.

TRACE BRANCH

Hazard

Trace Branch Recreation Area is in the back of beyond. It is not on the way to anywhere, nor is it easy to reach. Tortuously curvy roads try to find a way through Perry and Leslie counties toward Buckhorn Lake, which is an impoundment of the Middle Fork of the Kentucky River. And just when you begin to think Trace Branch is a figment of a mapmaker's mind, a road leads steeply down to a secluded, well-kept Army Corps of Engineers campground. And once you get here, there's not a whole lot to do except relax. Sure, you can swim, fish, and boat, maybe throw some horseshoes, or maybe not.

So why come to Trace Branch? For one thing, the price is right – free. You can also avoid the crowds. Being off the beaten path and unheralded keeps the campground empty. I would be surprised if all ten campsites have ever been occupied at the same time. There's hardly a soul here during the week. And in fall and winter, you can have it all to yourself. I doubt many people from more than 30 miles away have ever been here, no matter the season. And the locals, who are ultra-friendly, aren't about to divulge their little secret.

Here's the tale of the tape on Trace Branch. Drop down Moseley Bend Road and enter a picnic and boat launch area. A picnic shelter, convenient for rainy days, is in the central part of a grassy lawn. Next to

CAMPGROUND RATINGS

Beauty:	★★★★
Site privacy:	★★★
Site spaciousness:	★★★★★
Quiet:	★★★★★
Security:	★★★
Cleanliness/upkeep:	★★★★

Come here if you want to do nothing but relax.

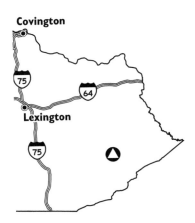

EASTERN

it is a playground for kids. A set of vault toilets, used by campers too, is beside the parking area. More picnic tables are set at the lake's edge. Dead ahead are the boat ramp and a small dock. Turn right and cross the tiny embayment of Trace Branch to enter the campground. To the left are two campsites on the Trace Creek embayment. River birch trees shade the picnic tables. Keep left around the loop and pass five more campsites strung along the banks of Middle Fork. A wooded ridge

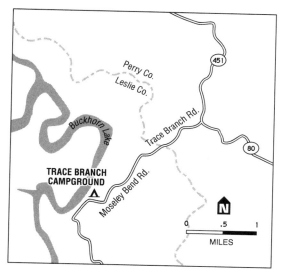

stands across the water. Tall river birch and willow trees shade most of these sites, but they still allow easy access to the water for boaters or swimmers. A grassy understory makes for soft tent sites, but it does little for privacy—if there were ever a lot of people here. The loop turns away from the river and passes two more shady campsites backed against a steep hill. A grassy field centers the loop. The only accouterment is a horseshoe pit. Remember to bring your own water.

So what to do? Fishing is an obvious choice. Campers bank-fish Buckhorn Lake for catfish, bass, and walleye right from their campsite. Boaters can launch their craft and tool down the lake. Very little private land on Buckhorn Lake ensures a scenic natural setting. Having few other boaters makes it even better. If you have a canoe, you can fish hard-to-access water upstream of the campground. Drive out of the campground and take a right, drive a short ways, then take the next hard right, which leads to a low-water bridge and the Confluence Recreation Area. Launch your boat upstream of the low-water bridge. Motorboats can't get upstream of here. These waters are accessible for bank fishermen, but you will be able to cover much more territory in a canoe.

Other than that, bring a good book. Bring a hammock. Bring your family. Bring a few friends. Maybe just bring your tent and a little food, then enjoy a few lazy days. After all, our high-tech life in the new millennium is passing fast enough.

To get there: From the junction of Mountain Parkway and KY 17 north of Hazard, head north on KY 17 for 5.5 miles to KY 28. Turn left on KY 28 West and follow it 6.2 miles to KY 451. Turn left on KY 451 South and follow it for 5.2 miles to Trace Branch Road. Turn right on Trace Branch Road and follow it as it turns into Moseley Bend Road at the Perry-Leslie County Line. Keep on Moseley Bend Road for 2.4 miles and the campground will be on your right.

KEY INFORMATION

Trace Branch
804 Buckhorn Dam Road
Buckhorn, KY 41721

Operated by: Army Corps of Engineers

Information: (606) 398-7251, www.lrl.usace.army.mil/bhl

Open: Year-round

Individual sites: 10

Each site has: Picnic table, fire ring, some have upright grills

Site assignment: First come, first served; no reservation

Registration: No registration

Facilities: Vault toilets (bring your own water)

Parking: At campsites only

Fee: None

Elevation: 780 feet

Restrictions:

  Pets—On 6-foot leash only

  Fires—In fire rings only

  Alcoholic beverages—At campsites only

  Vehicles—Maximum 2 vehicles per site

  Other—14-day stay limit

TURKEY FOOT

McKee

Normally shunning most camp-grounds on busy summer holidays, my experience and camping intuition told me that Turkey Foot would have sites available on the fourth of July. I was right, and I shared the 15-site campground with only two other groups. (For the sake of full disclosure, heavy thunderstorms were predicted for that day. And they did come, but the day was far from a complete washout.) Turkey Foot is neither near a big lake nor has obvious more-popular recre-ation opportunities. Rather, it is an old-fashioned campground where you make your own fun. And it wasn't hard, with the Sheltowee Trace Trail nearby and War Fork Creek for fishing.

In my opinion, the campground is just right. Cross a wet-weather bridge over War Fork Creek and enter the camp-ground. Head up a hill and come to the first two campsites nestled beneath a rich forest of hemlock, oak, and maple. A dense brushy understory grows among the trees. The campground road then levels off on a bench above War Fork Creek. Landscaping timbers and old-time rockwork make for level sites. Most of the campsites on the uphill side of the road are walk-ins with steps leading to them. The downhill side sites are closer to your car and are more oriented toward pure car camping. Thick woods and a lot of distance separate the sites, offering the most in campsite priva-

CAMPGROUND RATINGS

Beauty:	★★★★
Site privacy:	★★★★★
Site spaciousness:	★★★★
Quiet:	★★★★★
Security:	★★★
Cleanliness/upkeep:	★★★

Little-used Turkey Foot lies in a quiet part of the Daniel Boone National Forest on the banks of War Fork Creek.

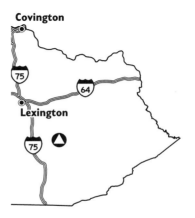

EASTERN

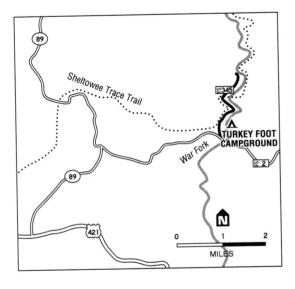

cy. The sites are generally spacious as well, offering plenty of room for even the most gear-laden tent camper. The curvy roads and lack of electrical hookups keep the big rigs away.

Keep down the campground road and notice that some of the walk-in sites are far enough uphill to remain unseen by other campers. About halfway along the gravel road are newer-style vault toilets. Come to the final site, number 15, just as the campground road drops back downhill to the Turkey Foot picnic area, which lies on a streamside flat overlooking War Fork. A field with a horseshoe pit is adjacent to the picnic area. Except for major holidays with clear weather, Turkey Foot campground fills infrequently. There are no reservations, no registration, and the price is right: free. And in this case you will get more than what you pay for. Come here for solitude on a holiday if you want a site. But remember you have to make your own fun.

I rolled in about noon, setting up my Eureka tent just as the skies were darkening. I took a little nap as the storm passed through, then walked the campground loop road while water dripped from the trees. The air had cooled to the 60s, so I decided to take a hike. Just across the campground bridge is a trail accessing Kentucky's master footpath, the Sheltowee Trace. I turned right and walked north for two miles, crossing Forest Road 345 a couple of times before dropping once again down to War Fork. The trail bisected War Fork here. Resurgence Cave stood on the left bank just at the crossing. The cave got this name from the water that flows from the dark cavern, filling the sometimes-dry streambed of War Fork. Fog hovered over the chilly water as it filled the streambed. Downstream were bluffs and other rock formations. This is also good fishing territory. In spring, War Fork is stocked with trout and offers angling for the cold water–loving fish and smallmouth bass.

If you want to see Resurgence Cave the easy way, take a right out of the campground on FR 345 and drive two miles. Look for a dirt road leading downhill to the right. There is a small parking area where the unmarked dirt road meets the Sheltowee Trace. Take the Trace downhill just a short distance to War Fork and the cave. War Fork is perennial below Resurgence Cave, but nice swimming pools flow at the Turkey Foot picnic area. Stone steps lead down to the water here. The Sheltowee Trace also leaves south from the campground and climbs the drainage of Middle Fork to reach Forest Road 376 after 3.7 miles. You probably won't see anyone on this section of trail, and you may not see anyone else at Turkey Foot for that matter.

To get there: From exit 76 on I-75 near Berea, head east on US 421 for 18 miles to McKee. Once in McKee, turn left on KY 89, passing through the town square. Follow KY 89 north for 3 miles to an acute signed right turn on paved Forest Road 17. Follow this paved road for 0.5 mile, turning left on a paved road which becomes Forest Road 2 after 1 mile. Continue forward on gravel FR 2 for 2 more miles to Forest Road 345. Turn left onto FR 345 and follow it 0.2 mile to the right turn into Turkey Foot.

KEY INFORMATION

Turkey Foot
761 South Laurel Road
London, KY 40744

Operated by: U.S. Forest Service

Information: (606) 864-4163, www.southernregion.fs.fed.us/boone

Open: Mid-April–mid-November

Individual sites: 15

Each site has: Picnic table, fire ring, lantern post, tent pad

Site assignment: First come, first served; no reservation

Registration: No registration

Facilities: Vault toilets (bring your own water)

Parking: At campsites only

Fee: None

Elevation: 900 feet

Restrictions:

Pets—On 6-foot leash only

Fires—In fire rings only

Alcoholic beverages—At campsites only

Vehicles—Maximum 2 vehicles per site

Other—No trash cans; pack it in, pack it out

YATESVILLE LAKE STATE PARK

Louisa

A new campground can be good in many ways. Obviously, the facilities will be in good shape and not worn down by troops of campers over decades of use. Being new lends a sense of being among the first to "discover" a new place. But the best aspect of the new campground at Yatesville Lake State Park is the good design. The architects who drew up this campground had obviously visited a few others and had listened to campers of all stripes. They came up with a camping area that suits the wants and needs of all types of state park visitors, from RV campers to boat campers to tent campers. The emerald green waters and tan stone bluffs of the Yatesville Lake were already here.

When you visualize the campground, imagine everything in tip-top shape. Pass the camper registration booth and stay right. Come to a well-manicured loop with 12 sites that have water and electricity. These sites are mostly grassy but have young trees planted that will provide adequate shade in the future. The sites are well separated and about the right size. The last three sites are all-accessible. This loop is almost nice enough to make me camp with the RVs here.

Pass the immaculate bathhouse with laundry facilities and enter the main section of well-dispersed sites. Most of them have young planted pines and hardwood trees shading them, with a few old maple trees

CAMPGROUND RATINGS

Beauty:	★★★★
Site privacy:	★★★★
Site spaciousness:	★★★★
Quiet:	★★★★
Security:	★★★★★
Cleanliness/upkeep:	★★★★★

Stay at one of Kentucky's newest and nicest state park campgrounds.

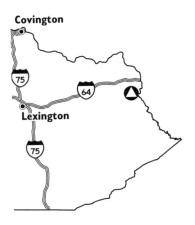

EASTERN

thrown in. Soon, you'll come to the walk-in primitive campsite parking area on the right. Follow a little gravel path to the first walk-in site, which is close. The next three sites are farther back in a mixture of shade and sun, heavy on the shade. Any of these four sites would make a tent camper happy. This design puts like-minded campers together. A hiker path continues down steeply beyond here to a gravel service road and the boat-in sites on Yatesville Lake. Even though these sites are offi-

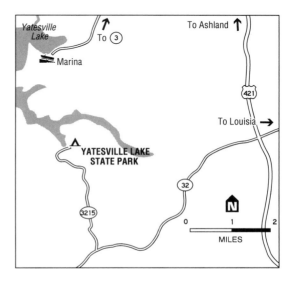

cially labeled boat-in, park personnel allow walk-in campers to use them.

Walk left along the gravel service road, and cut into the hillside below you are four superlative campsites. The lake is visible from these widely separated sites that are as private as you could want. Campsite B-1 is one of the best sites in the state, as it looks down the length of Yatesville Lake. To the right on the service road are four sites overlooking a cove and the lake. Keep on and come to seven more great campsites. The farthest one is a good half-mile from the walk-in parking area, but it's worth the hike. If you have a boat or canoe, these sites would be very easy to access from a boat launch just around the corner. The main campground has ten more campsites with water and electricity, of which any RVer would approve.

A fellow camper I visited with claimed Yatesville to be one of the best bass-fishing lakes in the east end of the state. The state of Kentucky claims Yatesville has the best bluegill fishing in the entire state. Largemouth bass, crappie, and catfish also ply the clear waters. Islands, bluffs, and scenic rock formation make even a fishless day a worthwhile outing. The park itself is split into two relatively small sections. The section with the campground, Pleasant Ridge, has five interconnected trails that wander along the lake and between the campground and the water. You will be using some of these if you walk to the boat-in sites.

The marina area has six interconnected trails, but it is a good ten miles distant. Get directions from park personnel at the campground. One path swings around the shoreline to the base of Yatesville Dam. A fishing pier and fishing lagoon make angling easy. A modern marina rents johnboats and pontoons. But with the great setting at Pleasant Ridge, you may never make it over there.

To get there: From exit 191 on I-64 near Ashland, head south on US 23 for 23 miles to KY 32 near Louisa. Turn right on KY 32 and follow it 4.7 miles to KY 3215. Turn right on KY 3215 and follow 2 miles to the campground.

Yatesville Lake State Park
P.O. Box 767
Louisa, KY 41230

Operated by: Kentucky State Parks

Information: (606) 673-1490, www.kystateparks.com

Open: April–October

Individual sites: 4 walk-in tent sites, 16 boat-in/walk-in lake sites, 27 water and electric sites

Each site has: Picnic table, fire ring, lantern post, tent pad; others also have water and electricity

Site assignment: First come, first served; no reservation

Registration: At campground entrance station

Facilities: Hot showers, flush toilets, vault toilets, water spigots, laundry, pay phone

Parking: At campsites and walk-in primitive site parking areas

Fee: $8.50 walk-in per night, $10 boat-in per night, $16 water and electric sites

Elevation: 590 feet

Restrictions:

Pets—On 6-foot leash only

Fires—In fire rings only

Alcoholic beverages—Not allowed

Vehicles—None

Other—14-day stay limit

APPENDICES

APPENDIX A
Camping Equipment Checklist

Except for the large and bulky items on this list, I keep a plastic storage container full of the essentials of car camping so that they're ready to go when I am. I make a last-minute check of the inventory, resupply anything that's low or missing, and away I go!

Cooking Utensils
Bottle opener
Bottles of salt, pepper, spices, sugar, cooking oil, and maple syrup in waterproof, spill-proof containers
Can opener
Cups, plastic or tin
Dish soap (biodegradable), sponge, and towel
Flatware
Food of your choice
Frying pan, spatula
Fuel for stove
Lighter, matches in waterproof container
Plates
Pocketknife
Pot with lid
Spatula
Stove
Tin foil
Wooden spoon

First Aid Kit
Band-Aids
First aid cream
Gauze pads
Ibuprofen or aspirin
Insect repellent
Moleskin
Snakebite kit
Sunscreen/chapstick
Tape, waterproof adhesive

Sleeping Gear
Pillow
Sleeping bag
Sleeping pad, inflatable or insulated
Tent with ground tarp and rainfly

Miscellaneous
Bath soap (biodegradable), washcloth, and towel
Camp chair
Candles
Cooler
Deck of cards
Fire starter
Flashlight/headlamp with fresh batteries
Foul weather clothing
Lantern
Maps (road, topographic, trails, etc.)
Paper towels
Plastic zip-top bags
Sunglasses
Toilet paper
Water bottle
Wool blanket

Optional
Barbecue grill
Binoculars
Books
Field guides on bird, plant, and wildlife identification
Fishing rod and tackle
GPS

APPENDIX B
Campground Information

**Big South Fork National River
and Recreation Area**
4564 Leatherwood Road
Oneida, TN 37841
(931) 879-4890
www.nps.gov/biso

Cherokee National Forest
2800 N. Ocoee Street
P.O. Box 2010
Cleveland, TN 37320
(423) 476-9700
www.southernregion.fs.fed.us/
cherokee

**Cumberland Gap National Historical
Park**
Box 1848
Middlesboro, KY 40965
(606) 248-2817
www.nps.gov/cuga

Daniel Boone National Forest
1700 Bypass Road
Winchester, KY 40391
(859) 745-3100
www.southernregion.fs.fed.us/boone

**Great Smoky Mountains National
Park**
107 Park Headquarters Road
Gatlinburg, TN 37320
(865) 436-1200
www.nps.gov/grsm

Kentucky Department of Tourism
P.O. Box 2011, Dept. WWW
Frankfort, KY 40602
(800) 225-8747
www.kentuckytourism.com

Kentucky State Parks
500 Mero Street
Frankfort, KY 40601
(800) 255-PARK
www.kystateparks.com

**Land Between the Lakes National
Recreation Area**
100 Van Morgan Drive
Golden Pond, KY 42211
(800) LBL-7077
www.lbl.org

Mammoth Cave National Park
Mammoth Cave, KY 42259
(270) 758-2328
www.nps.gov/maca

Natchez Trace Parkway
2680 Natchez Trace Parkway
Tupelo, MS 38801
(800) 305-7417
www.nps.gov/natr

Tennessee Department of Tourism
Rachel Jackson State Office Building
320 Sixth Avenue, 5th Floor
Nashville, TN 37243
(800) GO2-TENN
www.tnvacation.com

Tennessee State Parks
401 Church Street
L&C Tower, 7th Floor
Nashville, TN 37243-0446
(888) 867-2757 or (615) 532-0001
www.tnstateparks.com

INDEX

ABOUT THE AUTHOR

A native Tennessean, Johnny Molloy was born in Memphis and moved to Knoxville in 1980 to attend the University of Tennessee. It was there, on a backpacking foray into the Great Smoky Mountains National Park, that he developed a love of the natural world—a love that has become the primary focus of his life.

Though a disaster, that trip unleashed a passion for the outdoors that has encompassed more than 1,200 nights in the wild over the past 12 years. He has spent over 650 nights in the Smokies alone, cultivating his woodmanship and expertise on those lofty mountains.

After graduating from the University of Tennessee in 1987 and continuing to spend ever-increasing time in natural places, he became more skilled in a variety of environments. Upon suggestion and encouragement from friends, he began to parlay his skill into an occupation. The results of his efforts are numerous books: *Day & Overnight Hikes in the Great Smoky Mountains National Park* (Menasha Ridge Press, 1995 & 2001); *Trial by Trail: Backpacking in the Smoky Mountains* (University of Tennessee Press, 1996); *The Best in Tent Camping: Southern Appalachian and Smoky Mountains* (Menasha Ridge Press, 1997, 1999 & 2001), *The Best in Tent Camping: Florida* (Menasha Ridge Press, 1998), *Day & Overnight Hikes in Shenandoah National Park* (Menasha Ridge Press, 1998), *The Best in Tent Camping: Colorado* (Menasha Ridge Press, 1999 & 2001), *Day & Overnight Hikes in the Monongahela National Forest* (Menasha Ridge Press, 2000), *Mount Rogers Outdoor Recreation Handbook* (Menasha Ridge Press, 2001), *Hiking Trails of Florida's National Forests, Parks, and Preserves* (University Press of Florida, 2001), *Long Trails of the South* (Menasha Ridge Press, 2002), and *From the Swamp to the Keys: A Paddle Through Florida History* (University Press of Florida, 2002). Molloy has also written numerous articles for magazines such as *Backpacker* and *Sea Kayaker* and for websites such as gorp.com.

Today, Johnny continues to write about and travel extensively to all four corners of the United States, indulging in a variety of outdoor pursuits.